# the afterlife is a party

what people and animals
teach us about love,
reincarnation,
and the other side

## Robyn M Fritz

# the afterlife is a party

what people and animals teach us about love,
reincarnation, and the other side

Copyright © 2020 Robyn M Fritz

Published by Alchemy West, Inc.
Alchemy West Publishing
Seattle, WA 98116

All rights reserved. No part of this book except for brief quotations for review may be reproduced or transmitted in any form or by any means without written permission from the publisher.
Contact: robyn@robynfritz.com

**alchemywest**
balance • clarity • transformation

Alchemy West, Inc.
Robyn M Fritz MA MBA CHt, President

Design and Layout
Robert Lanphear, Lanphear Design

Copyeditor
Laurel Robinson, Laurel Robinson Editorial Services

Photographer
Mary Van de Ven

Library of Congress Control Number: 2019914553

ISBN (print): 978-0-9844287-4-8
ISBN (ebook): 978-0-9844287-5-5

In Honor of Our Beloveds
For our lost beloveds, human or animal, especially my own.
Until we meet again.

My parents:
Ray J. Fritz and Rosemarie Fritz

My animal family:
Maggie
Murphy Brown
Alki
Grace the Cat
And all those Tweety bantam chickens

# Contents

In the Beginning .......................................................................... 1
**Chapter 1**: The Biggest Problem You're Not Thinking About ......... 5
   *A Healing Story: Reconciling with Mom* ..................................... 11
**Chapter 2**: I Just Had to Be Me ................................................... 21
**Chapter 3**: Alive, Then Dead: What My Parents Did ................... 37
**Chapter 4**: The Gray Zone: Suddenly (or Not) You're Dead ......... 57
   *A Healing Story: Unexpected Healing* ........................................ 73
**Chapter 5**: The Way Stations for Dead Things
   on the Other Side ................................................................... 81
**Chapter 6**: More True Things About the Afterlife ....................... 97
   *A Healing Story: The Persistent Dead* ...................................... 111
**Chapter 7**: Walking the Mystery with Our Animal Families ....... 121
**Chapter 8**: How Energy, Culture, and Mindset
   Affect Our Lives—and Deaths .............................................. 157
**Chapter 9**: Energy, the Stuck Dead, and Us: Why It Matters ..... 173
**Chapter 10**: Getting Stuck (or Not):
   How We Mess Up, or Save, Our Afterlives ............................ 185
   *A Healing Story: Family Reunion* ............................................ 197
**Chapter 11**: Healing Grief and Moving On ............................... 209
Parting Words ........................................................................ 227
Acknowledgments ................................................................... 231
About the Author ................................................................... 233

# In the Beginning

If you want to know what really happens when we die—yes, what *really* happens—this is your book. You'll find out how the afterlife works from someone who started out as a reluctant medium and is telling it like it really is. Because it's time someone did.

I'm eager to share the truth about the afterlife because what I've learned is comforting, concerning—and absolutely true. Bottom line: the afterlife is a party. Yes, a party! I'm not kidding: I have proof of that from the dead themselves, especially my dad, Ray, who died in 1994.

Let me back up. I'm a professional intuitive who became a psychic medium because my deceased dad came back to visit, as most of our loved ones do—and then he decided to put me to work. You know what parents are like! But, dang it, he had a point: from his perspective in the afterlife he could see the living and the dead reaching for each other, trying to connect, anxious to heal grief and get closure. Plain and simple, he wanted to help. That desire led to his next soul choice, to run what I call a Way Station for Dead Things on the Other Side, where those who have just transitioned to the afterlife rest up before they figure out what to do next.

Dad's soul choice also led to me. To help the living and the dead connect, he decided I should be the psychic medium, sitting with clients eager to connect with their deceased human and animal beloveds, and he would bring the dead to chat with us. Not the guessing game kind of mediumship that seems to be the "in" thing these days, but honest-to-goodness real conversations.

That worked out really well, and continues to, but Dad also had another big idea: he wanted me to help the dead he couldn't help by himself—the stuck dead, those who aren't in the afterlife, the ones most of us don't even realize exist. That led to us busting the afterlife wide open, but in a good way!

I'm going to tell you a lot about the afterlife—what our human and animal beloveds are up to, how we can connect with them, even how and why they reincarnate—things you just won't get anywhere else. And I'm doing it with stories from the dead themselves, specifics about how the afterlife works, and fascinating transcriptions of actual mediumship sessions where both the living and the dead got closure—and surprised.

But here's something you need to know and deal with: yes, the afterlife is a party, and it really exists—but not everyone gets in. That's not just sobering, it's a serious problem that affects all of us, including the planet itself.

Let me explain. We're scared about dying, and worried about deceased loved ones, because we believe a story about death that isn't true. The truth is, we don't have to be religious to get to the afterlife, or even good. We just have to love ourselves unconditionally. And most of us don't—alive or dead.

That's not how it's supposed to work. The afterlife isn't set up for us to fail: it's set up for us to win, to be a step on our soul's journey from one incarnation, or life, through death and into another experience. Forever. Our souls know that. We just need to remember who we are, where we came from, and where we're going. That will help us succeed at the hard but necessary work of learning to love ourselves, which is the key to eternity. To be honest, before my dad showed up, I'd never thought about the afterlife, and self-love seemed to be something for other people. Now I know better, and as you read this book, so will you. I promise.

As I show you how the afterlife works, I'm going to spill all of it. Like:

- Self-love is the key to life—and death. Embracing love as our guiding principle helps us claim fearless, joyful, confident lives and wise deaths that lead to stunning new experiences that are, as my dad says (and he should know), "more than you could ever imagine or will imagine when you're inside a body."

- The afterlife requires a navigation system, and we must know how it works *before* we get there—or risk missing it. Luckily, it's a foolproof system: we just have to take advantage of it.

- What's keeping millions of the dead out of their afterlife isn't what you think. Blame some of that on doctrine: all those "places" religion and culture talk about don't exist, but thinking they do messes people up when they die.

- The stuck dead throughout history, yes, *history*, have unintentionally created an invisible energy block on the planet that has created a worldwide crisis, keeping the living and the planet from thriving, even preventing peace on Earth. The good news? I've figured out how to clear up that energy block, and I'm doing it, which means we can all live better lives on a healthy, vibrant Earth. Even better news? You can help—by learning to love yourself and by teaching your beloveds, alive or dead, how to claim self-love and keep moving forward.

I learned these truths about death and what comes next from working with my dad and talking with the dead, from those who successfully made it to their afterlives to those who didn't until we helped them. It's all here for you—to explore, to help you connect with your beloved dead, human or animal, and to even welcome them back, as I have throughout my life. Yes, the afterlife is real—and so is reincarnation.

This book will help you stop fearing death and in the process claim an exhilarating life, vibrant afterlife, and juicy new soul experience. It will help you learn to love yourself, no matter what. Because that's what you came here to do—and you deserve it. So let's get to it.

CHAPTER 1

# The Biggest Problem You're Not Thinking About

I asked my dad, Ray, who has been dead over twenty years, "What's the number one thing you want people to know about being dead?"

He laughed. "It's a constant party!"

Startled, I laughed, too, then cracked up when my soul mate dog, Murphy, who died in 2012, joined in, bragging about the raucous games the dead play together.

Hilarious, right? The afterlife is a party! Then my dad got serious.

> There's more, a lot more than you could ever imagine or will imagine when you're inside a body. It's further than you could ever go, which is for obvious reasons why you need your body to stop so your spirit can continue on. I didn't know it when I was in a body, and this is the most important thing, I would think, for somebody who is alive to know.

So there it is, in a happy nutshell: not only are our dead beloveds having fun (while missing us as much as we miss them), but they discover there's a universe of experiences waiting for them because they're no longer limited by their physical bodies. Puts a whole new spin on the "death and dying" thing, doesn't it?

Have you lost someone? Does it help to hear that our dead beloveds are having fun?

I found my dad's laughing commentary, and Murphy's enthusiasm, the most comforting things my beloved dead have ever said to me. It doesn't make me miss them less; in fact, I miss them more, because I want to have fun with them. However, it does make me smile, even if it's bittersweet.

Joining the afterlife party is something for us all to look forward to (*decades* from now). And if that was all there was to it, we'd all discover that when we die.

But there's a darker truth to the afterlife: it absolutely exists—but not everyone gets in. Why? Because we don't have to be religious to get there, or even good—we just have to know how, and most of us don't. That means we could miss it altogether.

Sadly, many people do. They are the stuck dead, the people who aren't having fun because they haven't made it to the afterlife party my dad raves about. Why are they stuck? Usually because they didn't know the truth about death and what comes next, so they weren't prepared for it. I know, because the stuck dead keep showing up at my house. Uninvited.

Granted, that's because I'm what some people call a psychic, or what I call a professional intuitive, a far cry from my former self, an executive MBA. Intuitives can choose many specialties, but my being a medium was actually my dad's idea. He showed up one day and asked me to help him help the dead, and kept at it until I agreed. Before that, I never considered mediumship, even though I've seen the dead since I was nine. What could they possibly have to say? They were dead—and gone. Except, apparently, at my house.

Most of us are like I was back then. We miss our dead, and might be curious about them, but we're busy living hectic lives, juggling all the things that make, break, please, or annoy us on any given day. We're likely to spout, "I'll worry about being dead when I'm dead." Which, as you're about to learn, would be dumb.

And the metaphysical types? They're preoccupied with that sensible old stumper, what we're supposed to do with our lives right now. What can the dead possibly add to that?

As it turns out, quite a lot. When we know the truth about death, we become more open to enjoying and celebrating life, rolling with the punches, taking grief in stride, and meeting death wisely. We're free to live, love, prosper, and have fun while learning what matters most: how to love ourselves first.

This is a critical point, because the biggest problem any of us will ever have is the one we're not thinking about. Yes, it's not knowing the truth about being dead—until we're dead.

Really. It absolutely astonishes me how so many people get through their lives—maybe not easily, but they at least get *through* them—and then they hit the very last step, being dead—and screw it up. Ironic, isn't it? Since we all die, you'd think we'd die well, instead of what many of us do: die badly.

Those who die badly don't easily move from dying to the Other Side; instead, they get stuck in a timeless in-between state and literally go nowhere, becoming what I call the stuck dead. They don't rest up from their lives, learn anything from them, or get to choose a new soul experience. That means the adventures of their eternal, timeless souls stop and they do nothing, often for years longer than the lives they just lived, until, and if, they somehow manage to move on to their proper afterlives. For these conflicted souls, death is the end of the game, and that is *not* what death is all about.

Death is actually the start of a new journey that begins the moment we die and continues when we safely move on to our proper afterlives, where we recuperate, review our lives, and eventually choose a new soul experience. That can include exploring new life by reincarnating in some form on Earth (or, yep, somewhere else) or in different dimensions in spirit. These are the dead who died well, and like most mediums, I work with plenty of them and their living loved ones.

This isn't a religious or spiritual concept—it is how life and death really work. Why don't we know this? Because nothing in our society teaches us the truth about being dead, and that messes up the living—and the dead.

The truth is that heaven, hell, purgatory, limbo, and their equivalents in non-Christian traditions—all the places we're encouraged or cautioned about—do *not* exist. Other places *do* exist, which means that the *idea* behind "heaven" is true, but the reality is so much better!

What *do* exist are places that seem truly magical, like Way Stations for Dead Things on the Other Side. (Yes, I've made up names for the places I see in the afterlife, names that describe their function, add a light note to a heavy subject, and are cheerfully accepted by the dead.) The way stations are places run by enlightened deceased people to support the dead immediately after they successfully transition to the Other Side. I know about them because my dad, Ray J. Fritz, runs one. In fact, his job was one reason why he asked me to help the dead—especially the stuck dead, the ones he couldn't help by himself.

The dead who have successfully made it to their proper afterlives are deciding whether, how, and when to reincarnate while exploring the universe, from hiking snowcapped mountains on alien planets to lounging in Hawaii, and, yes, checking in on loved ones left behind.

However, the stuck dead aren't having any adventures. They're stalled until they ask for or accept help or somehow figure out how to help themselves. They're often lost, lonely, resigned, even scared.

Believe me, your heart hurts when you meet a dead child who can't find her mom, a suicide who won't move on until he's understood, or the lost who feel doomed because nothing looks like what they were expecting. *My* heart hurt to hear their stories and to realize that not only are there billions of stuck dead, but people keep dying and getting stuck, so there clearly hasn't been a solution in play.

There is now, because my dad and I teamed up to create one. Once we did that, it didn't take long for me to see why he really wanted me to help the dead.

Telling the truth about death and what comes next would help the living embrace full lives—and wise deaths. Noble, huh? And something I could probably do, because I have what even I consider an annoying personality trait: I'm a maverick, someone who tends to dismiss current cultural "shortcomings," shall we say, in favor of what really works.

But there were still all those stuck dead, somebody had to help them, and my dad thought that "somebody" should be me. I grumbled a bit about pushy dead parents, but I was also curious, so I looked closer. We're taught to think about death in black-and-white religious terms (if at all), so we're usually expecting the judgmental afterlife that history has created. That means we aren't prepared for what really exists, so the newly dead often don't know what's going on or what to do, and are terrified they're about to be punished for any one of the countless "transgressions" that proved they were human. This happens so often that you and your loved ones could very well die and get stuck.

That's just wrong. Death isn't set up to be an obstacle course. In fact, the dead often *do* know what to do but let fear block them because, just like when they were alive, they don't love themselves. Getting to the afterlife is a choice: will we choose to love ourselves—or not? Choosing love is the easiest and yet, oddly, the hardest thing we ever have to learn. Alive or dead.

When I understood that, I knew my dad had another reason for asking me to help the stuck dead, whether human or animal (yes, animals have afterlives, too): he was concerned for me. Like most of us, I lacked the self-esteem and self-confidence to love myself, which meant that I, too, could end up leading an unfulfilling life, get stuck after death, and miss my afterlife—and all the future lives my soul could experience.

That's why I'm showing you what really happens when we die, why the dead get stuck (or not), and how loving ourselves helps us claim exhilarating lives, wise deaths, and new soul adventures—forever. When I accepted the job to change the thinking around life and death, I asked my dad to join me, saying, "Hey, you got me into this."

Dad chuckled and said, "Yep."

"We need to teach people what love really means in the world."

Dad laughed. "That's my girl," he said. "We're doing this together."

Yes, and here's our story: the truth about getting to the afterlife, and what it means to all of us.

At this point, you're probably wondering who the heck I am and how I became so different. I wonder that myself sometimes, so let me tell you what I know. But first, a healing story, to give you a taste of how a real mediumship session works.

A HEALING STORY

# Reconciling with Mom

What happens during a mediumship session? Find out in the four healing stories I've included for you. In these stories the dialogue is a transcription of actual client sessions, while descriptive text puts you right in the session. To help you distinguish between my commentary or paraphrasing and what the dead actually say to me, I've used italics where I repeat their words verbatim.

These healing stories demonstrate the sacredness of mediumship sessions. The living and the dead are grieving and seeking mutual healing and closure. Both sides may need to resolve a lifetime of mixed feelings, from loving devotion to hurt and anger. Sometimes they want one last chance to say goodbye—or to finally hear what their souls need them to hear, and know. Sometimes miracles occur, when everyone understands that we all make mistakes and can learn from them, that we love, regardless, and it's okay—and necessary—to move on.

Since I've cut straight to the heart of the session, note that I always begin by creating what I call sacred space. This means that the place we are in, whether in person or online, is a sacred container that is safe and dedicated to the work at hand.

I then call in everyone's spirit guides—my guides, my client's, and the dead's. We all have spirit guides, our etheric spiritual support team. They are either assigned to us from birth to guide our spiritual lives, much like the concept of spiritual allies in shamanism or guardian angels in the Christian tradition, or join us for various activities or life events.

Once we're clear about session goals, I get clients grounded and balanced in the space with me with a brief guided meditation using crystals. This helps them release the cares and busy-ness of the day and primes them for our session.

It also helps me determine how my clients' intuition works, so I can explain it to them. This boosts their confidence in their natural intuitive abilities and helps them create a ritual to later connect with their dead on their own (see Chapter 11). This is so important! For example, people often tell me they try to talk with their dead but don't hear anything, so they give up trying. That's tragic, especially because the real problem is that their intuition doesn't work that way, so they're trying to connect by talking when they may be better at intuitively seeing, feeling, or simply knowing things. Spending a few minutes showing them how their intuition works helps them put it to work correctly.

When sessions end and the dead have left us, I conclude with spiritual and grief support, including a healing and blessing for all, and close the sacred space.

Sessions can be a delicate balance. My first interest is always my living clients, who are growing their souls in their current bodies. However, I never pass up the chance to help my other clients—the dead—finally get whatever they need to get, because all souls matter, and I'm as no-nonsense as I am empathetic (just call me my father's daughter). Between me and my dad, things get resolved, which is the point.

As you read these stories, imagine that you're creating sacred space to achieve your own healing and closure—and that your dead beloveds are joining you.

## Reconciling with Mom

Karen came to settle her feelings with her mother, Helena. Karen is a confident and skilled special education teacher, but as she walked in, she looked worried and hunched her shoulders, as if bracing for bad news.

Although Karen had worked hard to instill self-confidence in her daughter and granddaughter, she had struggled for years with a lack of self-worth and hurt feelings, which she felt like physical pain. Her mother, Helena, had been a difficult person, bipolar, aggressive, and mean. As she was dying, she apologized to Karen's brothers for her bad behavior, but not to her. Karen came to get closure by understanding her mother's behavior, but she dreaded being hurt again.

As she explained this, my dad, who had joined us from his way station, nodded at me, and I knew he would be Karen's staunch supporter. Then he brought Helena to join us. She was angrily waving her arms and swearing up a storm.

Startled, I looked at Karen and laughed. "She's here and she's swearing!"

"Yes, she swore all the time."

"She says, *'It's about damn time!'* So she's been wanting to talk with you." I addressed Helena. "Okay, you can talk, but let Karen speak first."

Karen's voice got quieter as she intently leaned forward. She took a deep breath and asked, "Why did she apologize to my brothers about her behavior but not to me?"

I looked at my dad, who was shaking his head, and Helena, who was glaring at me. As I turned back to Karen, I frowned.

"It's that age-old thing, male and female. She says men need everything spelled out for them. *'I always had to do extra to please them, to keep them in line, to make them listen to me. I didn't need to do that with you. You're the other part of me. I see now maybe you needed that, and I didn't do it. And I didn't want to say goodbye to you, and I'm not going to now, either.'* Okay, then, that's pretty clear!"

Surprised, Karen sat back in her chair. I noticed something else about her mom.

"She's with you more than she should be, in my opinion. And now she's yelling at me. Yeah, it's my opinion, Helena! My dad is standing back, because she's really mad at me, and he's getting out of the line of fire, so to speak."

I laughed and Karen giggled.

I raised my eyebrows at my dad, a clear heads-up, and he warily glanced at Helena and backed away. I said to Helena, "You know, there are other things to do in the afterlife besides hang around your kids and poke them in the back and stuff like that."

I looked askance at Karen, gauging her reaction. "Yes, I'm being an ass, but she can handle it," I said. I turned back to Helena. "You can travel anywhere, a planet or dimension." She objected and I pushed on. "Yes, I am being practical. You don't have a body—you can do anything you want. But hanging around your kids all the time?"

Karen was relaxing now, and chuckling at me. I rolled my eyes at her.

"Someone else is coming forward, and my dad is, too, again. Is it your dad? A very soft personality. I'm getting an energetic impression of a soft, mild-mannered personality, and that your mom was the general of the family."

"My dad, Mac," Karen said. "So then they're both here."

I nodded.

"Mom wrote a book. She didn't know I read it."

"She does now!" I exclaimed, watching Helena glower and my dad wisely step back again.

Karen said her mom being bipolar had been very hard on them all.

I nodded. "Actually, your dad is stepping in front of her. Yes, you did separate from Helena, I'm saying to him. There's a whole lot of stuff going on here, Karen. I'm just trying to get through the filters to get to what's important. Your dad is acknowledging problems with men and women in our culture. But your mom also came from a very powerful line of witches, and he didn't understand that. He did know you were very soft and damaged, and he didn't know how to handle that. It's not something he was good at."

"That sounds right," Karen said.

"Your mom saw that in you and didn't like it—the line of witches you're descended from, what we call intuitives or psychics. The women in your family aren't tapping these abilities and using them. You also don't feel like you're part of the regular world because you're not. It's not a culturally accepted thing. That's why I'm one of those out there saying it's normal, we are all intuitives and healers, and some of us are just better at it than others. I can't change the oil in my car. I can barely use a screwdriver. I got that from you, Dad!"

I laughed at him as he sheepishly raised his hands, admitting it.

"Your dad is saying he recognized something different about you but didn't know what it was. He's talking about the line of witches. And you're upset and depressed about your parents not valuing you. It's totally normal and correct. Just because they were parents does not mean they're role models."

Karen sighed. "I'm trying to be better than that."

"And you are. Your mom is looking at their lives. Your parents had past lives together and didn't work it out then or now. Your dad saw something that made you different and vulnerable, especially to her. She's very much of the mindset of the people who persecuted witches, even though she's descended from them, and now she's on the Other Side and realizes it, and says, *'I screwed that up.'* She's learning."

I handed Karen one of my newly acquired crystals, a druzy black amethyst. As she held it, I watched, fascinated, as it worked on her just like a human energy healer would, removing the energy lines between Karen and Helena so they were no longer connected. Karen's hands shook, and I urged her to hang on tight, because it was helping her heal.

"Just because they're our parents doesn't mean they were great matches for us. Your mom could never put her finger on it, only that you were like your dad's side of the family, and she didn't like it. Your personality, I mean—you took after him. She's getting an eye-opener, but she's not completely through her life review. She's evaluating her life. A bit resistant. She's saying, *'If I go through this whole thing and find out I'm not the best person in the world, I'm not going to be very happy.'*

"But what's the best person, Karen? You do the best you can with what you have, with the crap people put in your head and your own bad attitude, which may be a good attitude to someone else. It was a bad attitude to you and me, but to her it was 'No, you're not going to be like that—shape up! Not a little wimp.' In her opinion it was cut and dried, she was in charge, you're not gonna be like your dad's side of the family. Not a little wimp."

"She did say he was a wimp," Karen said softly, reeling a bit in shock.

I winced. "There you go. Sometimes I could be more diplomatic."

"But he married someone like him. My stepmother, Sally. It was a happy relationship."

As she said that, a woman walked into the way station, waved forward by my dad. She went to stand by Karen's dad, Mac.

"Oh, hello," I said. "Here she is—your stepmother. She says, *'If I could have been your mother, I would have. I feel like you're the daughter of my heart.'* She looks at your mother and says, *'Just for the record, you're an asshole.'* She's not holding it back!"

I laughed, and my dad nodded at me.

Touched that her stepmother, Sally, was so loving, Karen laughed. "Yeah, that's right, she would have said that."

"Your mom said, *'Yeah, I'm getting that.'* She says she's sorry, she doesn't completely understand the whole thing. She hopes that when you die, you can sit down and work it out. And your stepmom is looking at her, like, yeah."

Karen chuckled. "I felt very close to my stepmother."

"You create your family, Karen, and you've done that with your own kids. Just because they were your parents doesn't mean they had all the answers, and that generation did not. They went through the Depression and a world war, and expected with all that that nothing would go wrong. But it does."

"Yes, it does." Karen slumped in her chair.

"So your mom is like, she wasn't the right match for you, and not in previous lifetimes, either. This lifetime you came in thinking you could help her, and you found out it wasn't possible, because they have to meet you halfway, and she thought she was in charge because she was the mom. But she was scared."

Karen was surprised. "Scared?"

"That time period, they were told to go to work during the war and then had to give their jobs away when it ended. They were never valued. They had children, but how could they value them when they couldn't value themselves? Your mom has hardcore anger, layers of wood around her heart, and she is just not letting that go. Her spiritual team is working on it."

I paused to give us both a breather.

"Why did those souls choose to come into bodies?" I asked. "We can't solve their problems for them. We can feel bad about how they treated us, but your stepmom is saying you're better than that. They're all sorry, it really did damage you emotionally, and yet your spiritual team is saying you're such a bright light that your mom couldn't look at you in those moments. She was clairvoyant, meaning she could see things intuitively. She didn't acknowledge it, but she says that she'd look at you and see this bright light, and then couldn't look at you. It made her angry. It's too bad, but that's her problem, not yours! You're shining your light in your family and taking care of these kids, and it's beautiful! And she's acknowledging that. *You turned out well despite me.* It's the closest you'll get to an apology from her. You're sensitive. Your intuition runs toward feeling things, so be aware of that. It can hurt more because of that."

We then talked with a few of Karen's close friends who had recently died. I also did more energy healing to make sure all the attachments to her mom were gone, so she could start to recover in mind, body, and spirit.

"What else do you need for closure?" I asked her. "Your mom was not sick. She was a mean son of a bitch."

"She'd scream at me," Karen said, shuddering.

"She was mean. Just mean. Even your dad and stepmom are saying the same thing. You don't get excused because you're sick or have a mental illness or a heart issue. You make the best of it, and she didn't. She thought she was better than everyone, and anything that looked weak she was going to go for the throat.

"I'm not being critical of your mom. It sounds like it. I'm just describing what I'm told was her personality. We can go through our entire lives allowing ourselves to get beat up by what happened, but the truth is you are this incredibly beautiful person and you deserve better."

Karen smiled shyly at me. She looked relieved, and actually younger than when she arrived for our session. Getting the pain out can do that. But she needed a deeper explanation, and Helena's spiritual team gave it.

"We take bodies to grow our souls," I said. "Sometimes we don't grow like we could have. One way your mom could have grown is being pointed out by her spiritual team. She did start out trying to understand the softer, gentler personalities, which is why she married your dad—on a level she didn't really connect with emotionally. She was attracted to it. Then she thought it wasn't tough enough for the world, and she was determined to make everybody as tough as possible, not understanding that you're tough like you are. You didn't have to be a mean or rigid personality.

"She said she apologized to your brothers and not you, but in a sense she is doing that now. But she still thinks that if a woman gets any sort of acknowledgment about being soft, she's not done her job about being tough. That's why she's withholding that apology. She's ignoring us all, so that's as far as we're going to get."

I stopped to listen as Helena's spiritual team changed the subject.

"So, Karen, remember what I said earlier, your mom is always hanging around the family? She's talking to your six-year-old granddaughter. Did you know that? It sometimes looks like these kids have invisible playmates. I'm going to discourage that. Here's what I think. We take Helena completely away from her, so she's not in your granddaughter's energy field. Then we replace her with a softer spirit guide."

Unnerved to learn that her angry, dead mother had been spending time with her granddaughter, Karen agreed. I paused as the granddaughter's spiritual team stepped forward and the softer guide took Helena's place. It was that easy.

"Good—they just did that. Now talk to your granddaughter in the coming days. Say, 'Do you know you have this soft, wonderful guardian angel?' Then support this spirit guide. She's soft, not obtrusive. Be gentle and matter-of-fact about it with your granddaughter. She's highly intuitive and sensitive, like all the women in the family."

Karen lit up, delighted with the soft spirit guide.

"Now, listen." I wanted this grieving, gentle woman to see how amazing she was, to let go of the pain. "It's your mom's problem, not yours. Look at what a beautiful family you have, the beautiful person you are. You did that by yourself. Thank yourself for that, and your dad and stepmom. They're saying they helped. Just because you're born to them doesn't mean your parents were the best match for you. You have to create your own family, and you did. Your mom hears you!"

I finished the energy healing work, and Karen handed me the black amethyst she'd been holding.

"I drew out the last of your mom's attachment to you," I said. "It's done with. You have made a beautiful life. When we look between lives in past life regressions, it's amazing how many mistakes we make! We think we can help others, but it gets messed up. So go off, be with the family you created, and be at peace over your mom. It's over."

Karen smiled and relaxed. She was exhausted, but beginning to look like she had found some closure after years of doubt. She had also learned how important her life was—to her and to her family. She realized that she had loved herself all along, no matter how her mother made her feel. She left with a bounce and a smile, feeling whole and complete, relieved to have made peace with her difficult mother and to know her father and stepmother were still looking out for her.

**The Point:** Sometimes talking with our dead can help us resolve the pain we suffered during our lives with them and move on with grace, determination, and love.

CHAPTER 2

# *I Just Had to Be Me*

I was obsessed with death as a child. Piously obsessed, that is. According to Catholic doctrine every November 2 was All Souls' Day, when we could slip into any Catholic church, say a few prayers, and spring a sad soul from purgatory.

Since praying was the one thing girls could excel at in that culture, and I was fiercely competitive, I relished the opportunity to shine while being useful. So on All Souls' Day I'd gulp lunch, run into our coldly imposing church, spout earnest if hurried prayers, race out so a soul would be freed, and charge back in to do it all over again until the school bell rang. Each "trip" launched one suffering soul out of purgatory and into heaven on the one day a year that could happen. I counted my "saves" while also wondering how the system worked: who got sprung, who died, and how I got credit for my saves. Did I say I was competitive?

Yep, and also confused. The nuns claimed the dead needed help because everybody got stuck in purgatory, so why was I alone in church? I was almost in high school before I realized I might be missing something.

I certainly was, but with good reason. When I was nine, my fourteen-year-old brother, Randy, died of leukemia—on November 1. Saving souls from purgatory on November 2 was my weird grief therapy, how I found meaning in something that has none—the death of a sibling. Since it hurt to think

Randy might be in purgatory, I tried to make sure he wasn't, and expected any leftover prayers to free other souls. I hated the rules and, born proactive, went for the solution: I prayed the dead out of trouble.

Now I smile and bless that naïve, repressed, and faithful child who bridled at Catholic rules yet still rallied to do the right thing. She was authentic—and an idiot.

Yes, helping the dead mattered to me even way back when. Yet even though they were quite real to me, I never expected to actually see a dead person in spirit. That happened for the first time a few days after my brother died, when he briefly appeared to me in a brilliant bubble of light. My grieving family both believed me and grilled me on the details. Considering their strong cultural and religious bias against taking females seriously, that was remarkable. And wishful thinking: they thought my seeing Randy meant he was a saint. In truth, it was simply the first time I saw the dead.

Other things happened that were more difficult to explain and live with. I would wake up at night and see things I thought were ghosts standing beside my bed. I'd huddle, terrified, as they bent down to cup my face in their see-through hands. Now I know they were my spirit guides as we know and discuss them today, and other beings who were aware that I could communicate with them and came to check me out, including the dead. Sadly, I was too frightened to respond to them.

Two years later I was alone with my beloved great-grandmother as she was in the hospital, dying. Suddenly the room filled with a bright light and she opened her eyes, smiled at the doorway, and said her family was there. Although I didn't see anyone, I could clearly feel that the room was suddenly stuffed full of ... something. She glowed as she relaxed, and remained peaceful until her death several days later.

Add to that my ability to know what animals were thinking

and to prefer the company of an old-growth forest to people, and you can see why my family thought I was a very strange child—something my dad points out even now, more than two decades *after* he died. Nowadays parents might intervene with psychological treatment, which is, ironically, why being female most likely saved me—I was irrelevant. My parents shrugged off my strangeness and I just went on being me, completely unaware that no one else was having my experiences, or that they were "peculiar."

Like most children, especially back then, I grew up and forgot my mystical childhood and "real life" got in the way. I loved learning, so I earned way too many college degrees; I loved romance, so I got married; I loved my independence, so I got divorced; and I loved the Pacific Northwest where I grew up, so I moved home after a ten-year stint in Michigan and set out on a new career.

I salvaged one thing from my marriage: my beloved English cocker spaniel, Maggie. We moved back to Oregon together, and after her untimely death, I noticed she was still around. I heard her barking in the house and in the yard, her toenails clicking on the floor, her feet thudding on the bark-padded yard, running like she hadn't run in years. Occasionally I saw her in wispy form as she raced back and forth, clearing the space. Yes, the space, for even though I didn't know anything about space clearing back then, my mom and I had frequently seen what we called ghosts in that house, and several weren't friendly. When the sounds of Maggie barking and racing through the house ended, the ghosts were gone.

I had long since abandoned religion, even spirituality, which I saw as a vaguely amusing and somewhat embarrassing intellectual exercise. But even though spirituality was not in my frame of reference, Maggie was. We adored each other, so while I had serious doubts about religion, I never had any about the world with Maggie in it. In our ten years together, we had just one minor glitch: she simply couldn't fetch a ball. I'd throw it, she'd chase it—and then wait for me to fetch it and throw it again.

I'd never thought much about reincarnation, either as a spiritual concept or something I'd actually do. I'd certainly never thought about my dog doing it, so even as I said it that day in Michigan, about three years before Maggie died, I wondered where the thought came from. Laughing at yet another fetching failure, I hugged her close and said, "Maggie, I love you, but if you ever decide to come back to me, please be able to fetch."

After Maggie's death, it was twelve years before my next dog showed up. She was an eleven-week-old Cavalier King Charles spaniel who eventually chose Murphy as her name. On our first morning together I threw a ball for her, and when she fetched it and dropped it in my lap, I suddenly remembered what I'd asked of Maggie so many years before. Perplexed, I gawked at Murphy as she cockily looked me in the eye and grinned. It still took me almost three years to figure out that the soul I adored in Maggie was back in a new body. (Sometimes you're just ... slow.)

But in those twelve years between dogs, I wasn't just dog-less: I was also nearly life-less. I had left Michigan ready to fling myself into a high-powered business career. After all, what else would a newly minted MBA do?

I have no idea, because I suffered a devastating injury and failed surgery that sparked disability and chronic illness. I was out of the workforce for years. For fifteen years I couldn't work at all. In the years when everyone else builds a future, mine disappeared.

## Ready or Not, Here Comes My Life

Despite all the depressing crap in my life, I still had a sense of humor, and although I didn't quite realize it, I also wanted to love and be loved. That's how Murphy, my wily Cavalier King Charles spaniel, came into my life—and that's when everything changed. In the years that followed, I learned what love meant (it's tough, no-nonsense, and the foundation of the pioneering, visionary mindset I teach). I also became an intuitive, what I call a conversationalist, or what others would call a crackpot or psychic medium. Above all, I'm a true-blue American, which means I have to blame this strange turn on someone else, so I will. I blame the dog—and the earthquake.

I knew Murphy was unusual right from the start. Yes, she had freaky street smarts, but the clincher came on February 28, 2001, when she alerted me to the 6.8 magnitude Seattle earthquake minutes *before* it hit. Astounded, I realized I was living with a scientific breakthrough: humans can't tell us when an earthquake is coming, but my dog could, and did. *And* had acted to save both our lives.

That's when I began to remember my unusual childhood. The mindset that we are guardians and caretakers in charge of the world has dominated world history, even in societies mostly aware of the living world around them. I never quite bought that theory, even as a child. To me, everything was alive and equal, but I also couldn't explain it, I just knew it. Then Murphy arrived.

Fascinated by her response to the earthquake, I decided to find out what was really going on in the world. I put on a science-y hat, and when that didn't explain things, I put on an intuitive one as well. The human-centric worldview exploded as I rediscovered a living, aware universe and something else I'd lost in childhood: telepathy. As Murphy and I explored our lives together, my intuitive abilities, largely dampened since childhood, awakened.

In 2004 I began having conversations with beings I had no idea could, or would, talk with us (and, come on, neither did you)—animals, trees, plants, hurricanes, earthquakes, volcanoes, oil spills, nature guardians, homes, and businesses. Even now, when intuitives are as mainstream as, well, scientists, my experiences are unique. A talking car that insisted it was mine and prompted me to send three dealers on a five-state search for it? I found it, and it is still the family car today. A rumbling volcano with a strong desire to show off by erupting? We talked, and Mount St. Helens changed her mind.

My life was fun, hilarious, moving, and, frankly, so disturbing that I did what any logical, skeptical person would do: I went to my neurologist to rule out insanity or a brain tumor. He smiled benignly and told me I was normal (for me). With that I declared myself free to get on with it, whatever "it" was. I established an intuitive practice that, true to my (annoying) maverick DNA, includes my own method of intuitive consultation and energy healing. That came about with the assistance of my business partner, Fallon—a crystal ball.

## The Coming of Fallon

Very few normal things seem to happen in my life. I'd worry about that, but what exactly is normal? Not even science can explain gravity and aspirin, yet we take them both for granted: they fit our experience, which is what works for us. That's why I tell myself to not be surprised by anything, even though I routinely am.

Fallon, the Citrine Lemurian Quartz, came into my life in 2009 (or back into my life, since I remember many lifetimes with him). Fallon is an ancient power crystal, a healer and a truth bringer—and my business partner. He is one of the amazing beings who has come back into the world at a time of tremendous growth and change. In his own words (yes, everything can talk with us), he says he is "a gift from the earth to its people."

His combination of citrine and Lemurian quartz is rare, but

what makes him Fallon is unique. The ancient crystal skulls, which are the only power crystals you usually hear about, are computers. Fallon is not a computer: he is a crystal who can, and does, bring real magic back into the world. Without him, a lot of the discoveries I've made and methodologies I've created might not even exist, from how I clear spaces to how I can help hundreds of thousands of the stuck dead move to the afterlife at once, in only a few minutes.

If you find this surprising, it's only because we think of using crystals for intuitive insights as "woo-woo" while depending on them for technological advances like computers. Please, get over yourself: I did, so I know it's possible.

Fallon and I are one of the emerging equal partnerships between people and other beings—in this case, crystals. We remember previous lifetimes together. Here's what led to our reunion in my current lifetime.

One day, I think in 2005, I was driving home from Portland, Oregon, when I started talking with a group of beings who showed me an ancient past life with a tool or talisman that I had misused and so put away until I remembered how to love. They said that this "talisman" was my partner, and that the time had come: my partner was coming back to me. I could see it: it was a bright yellow-white light.

Meanwhile, Fallon had bounced around the world for years. Nobody would buy him because no one could understand or work with his energy. He finally ended up in Brazil, where they carved him into an eight-pound crystal ball and sold him to a U.S. crystal expert who recognized his unique nature and put him in her personal collection. The only time he was ever out in public was when she took him to a crystal class she taught in Seattle six years later.

My analytical, skeptical side teamed up with my curious, open-minded side and went with me to that crystal class that day. See, I get how hard it is for people to get past the stereotype of a "crystal ball" and take one seriously, because when she invited the class to work with it, I thought, *For crying out loud, she brought a crystal ball. How weird is that?* Embarrassed, but a good sport, I played along.

As I picked up the crystal ball and gazed into it, I immediately zipped off to an etheric place above the planet that I'd long been working in and never consciously visited. Plus, all the beings I'd been talking with the last few years, including those who had told me my partner was coming back, were in the crystal smiling back at me. All of them. And by that time, I knew that many of them were multi-dimensional beings that aren't here on this planet. Yes, the *A*-word, as in "aliens" (I know what that sounds like).

I had just met my partner. He wasn't a symbol or a talisman or a light in my head. Criminy—he was a crystal ball. I took a deep breath and asked him if he was ready to be with me. He was. But was his "owner" ready to let him go?

She was not. I tried to buy him at the end of the class, knowing it was a sacred moment. The crystal was a conscious, living presence and my partner, but she wasn't ready to let him go. I waited for months while talking with him telepathically. That's when he told me his name was Fallon.

I said how concerned I was that he was a crystal ball now, a different shape than the one I knew him in centuries ago. Would we be able to work together? Was he "ruined"? He grumbled, saying, "Well, you're not the tall blond woman I knew back then, either." That made us both laugh. It would be all right. Nine months later the crystal expert was ready to sell. Fallon came home in December 2009, and a year later we opened our intuitive practice.

Please note: Fallon is not a being in a crystal, he *is* the crystal, just like I am human. He is alive, aware, a real personality, equal. Because we humans have only been in our bodies a short time, and he's been in his for eons, he can easily access wisdom we've forgotten. And does.

He is not my tool, and I am not his guardian or caretaker. An equal partner in our work, he has a say in what we do together, and no hesitation about saying it. I listen because we're partners and that's what partners do. He keeps me safe in my work, and when we work with my dad and the dead, his energy helps boost the connection.

## Some Early Mediumship Experiences

When Fallon showed up and changed everything, I was already bumbling around the intuitive realms, exploring what was out there. Wouldn't you know there'd be a catch? The last thing I was interested in was talking with the dead, but as my intuitive abilities blossomed, that's who started showing up. Here are a few stories of my early experiences with the dead—and what they teach us.

### A Family Member's Dad

I was in my own session with a respected psychic in the spring of 2006 when my cousin's dad, Lucas, who had died unexpectedly a few days earlier, suddenly showed up. He was standing in a foggy place (that I now call the Gray Zone), and asked what was going on. When I explained that he was dead, he was quite upset. He didn't want to be dead, and he was unprepared and alone: his spirit guides weren't there!

Stunned, I yelled for Lucas' team, and they abruptly appeared, saying they'd been looking for him since he died. I didn't know spirit guides could lose their people when they die, but they can—and do. Doesn't that just suck? Lucas' team took over and helped him move on while promising to bring him back for his funeral to say goodbye to his family. I know he did, because I saw and felt him there.

**The Point:** Death is sometimes disorienting for our spiritual teams. They aren't all they're cracked up to be, so pay attention, and when you wake up dead, be prepared to help yourself.

### Rusty the Dog: (Almost) a Journey to the Afterlife

One day in early 2007 my friend Ann called. Her dog, Rusty, an eleven-year-old shepherd mix, had suddenly become violently ill and was undergoing an emergency splenectomy. She asked me to find out what was wrong.

When I connected with Rusty, I saw fiery red dots in his blood, and told Ann I suspected terminal cancer. Sadly, a few days later the pathology report confirmed it: Rusty was dying.

During the next few weeks I got the brilliant idea that if Rusty was ready, I could help him move on. With Ann's permission, I connected with him to see what I could do.

Suddenly I was astral traveling (which means your etheric body travels somewhere while your physical body remains behind). Rusty and I were standing inside a large, rocky cave. Ann's etheric body hovered uncertainly behind us, and before us was a narrow stone bridge leading to the cave's entrance. Outside, Ann's deceased mother and dog urged Rusty to join them.

Rusty stared morosely at them, glanced back at Ann, and hesitated. Thinking he was ready to die but needed help, I decided to escort him to the Other Side. (We can all be goof-ups in our own special way.)

"Come on, Rusty," I said. "I'll walk with you to the cave entrance, so you don't have to be alone, and then you can decide what to do."

We stepped onto the stone bridge together. Rusty was walking ahead of me, and I had taken only a few steps when a man yelled, "Robyn, no! You can't do that!" and tackled me, knocking me headfirst off the bridge. I had enough time to see Rusty turn back and return to Ann before our connection broke and I was back at home, the astral journey over and my body physically aching from the tackle (which isn't supposed to be possible, but I guess I'm just a psychic anomaly—or a klutz).

The man was one of my many spirit guides (mine are androgynous warrior giants, because I'm apparently prone to doing silly things and need regular interventions). My guides scolded me, saying that if I had crossed that bridge, my physical body would have died. Clearly that was a bad idea, and I haven't tried it again. Even I occasionally learn from my mistakes.

Rusty lived a few weeks longer. Ann and I were with him when he died, and I was relieved to see Ann's deceased family greet him in the afterlife.

**The Point:** The road to the afterlife is one we all have to walk alone, even if we're part of a crowd. All the living can do is say farewell.

### Raymond the Bear and Ralph the Deer: Unlikely Best Friends

Fast-forward to 2009–2010. My good friend Jody, who was my dog Alki's breeder, is my animal family's honorary Grandma Jody. She was living in a small Northern California mountain town when her intuitive abilities opened up. One day she saw a big buck in a meadow who, as she telepathically chatted with him, said his name was Ralph. Shortly afterward, Jody leaped out of bed in the middle of the night when a huge black bear raided her garbage can; he said his name was Raymond.

Jody and I were soon chatting regularly with them. A lasting friendship was forged between the four of us, especially between the animals themselves, who, despite their obvious species differences, soon considered themselves best friends.

Of course, things changed. One morning I was restless and uneasy, hearing a sound, like whispering, until I finally heard: "Ralph is dead." I immediately called Jody, and we connected with Ralph. He had been chased by coyotes into the mountains and broken his leg. He lay in the rocks for several days, calling for us, but we never heard him, and he died alone. As we grieved, Raymond joined us in saying goodbye.

Over the next few months Jody and I talked with Ralph the Deer—he was our first in-depth connection with the dead. He told us how amazing being dead was, including how wild animals are well cared for by people in comfortable buildings and on open land where they get to eat as much as they want and wander around making new friends. Ralph was having a great time, but he missed Raymond—and Raymond dreadfully missed him.

Some weeks later Dice, one of Jody's dogs, became antsy, a sign we'd learned meant he knew someone was going to die, a dubious talent if you visit hospitals and nursing homes, which Jody and her dogs did. Worried that Dice might be tapping into her ailing mother, Jody called me to check.

"No, it's Raymond," I said, after a brief pause to listen. "He's dying."

We immediately connected with Raymond, intuitively seeing him slumped beside a fir tree deep in the woods. Hungry and tired, he missed Ralph and was ready to die.

The next thing we saw astonished us: Ralph the Deer in his spirit form strolled into the woods and knelt down beside Raymond. He gently told Raymond how wonderful it was "over there," how they would get to eat their fill and finally be together.

As I tearfully watched, I was stunned to see my dog Maggie, who'd died years before, walk up to them. By then I knew she was part of my family's soul group in the afterlife, and that my dad called her "the little one." Now she waited quietly beside

Raymond the Bear and Ralph the Deer and I was awed to see her.

As Maggie stood watch, Jody and I said farewell to Raymond as he died peacefully, with Ralph snuggled next to him. Then they stood up together, transformed. Ralph was already a strong, big buck in the afterlife, no longer crippled, and Raymond was now vibrantly healthy. Amazed, I watched them walk off into the woods, with Maggie trotting alongside.

The scene shifted to a high mountain meadow with long green grass surrounded by fir trees, and people gathered around a picnic table enjoying a meal. In the distance Raymond and Ralph walked out of the woods, side by side, with Maggie trailing.

A man whose back was to me got up and walked into the meadow to watch. Hands on his hips, he leaned forward and laughed.

I was startled to hear him say, "Only my daughter would send a bear and a deer!" I peered closer, and sure enough, it was my dad—considerably younger and more vibrant than the crippled, aged man he'd been when he died.

Although I was delighted, I didn't understand exactly what my dad and Maggie were doing in the afterlife. I just knew that reality was far more complex than I had ever imagined, and I was lucky enough to catch a glimpse of it and see them!

Raymond and Ralph now live at my dad's way station and share in our work with the dead, especially with animals who need help transitioning. Unfortunately even dead people are alarmed by big black bears, so they frequently ask, *"Why is there a bear here?"* Since Raymond's feelings are easily hurt, we make sure he feels respected and needed even when he has to stand back so the human dead can comfortably join my dad. After they're settled in, they accept him. The animal dead have no problem with him, and see both Raymond and Ralph as playmates.

**The Point.** The afterlife is complex and well organized. As my dad says, "There are places for everything that dies," from humans to animals, buildings, and vegetation—you name it. All beings are welcome and treated equally and respectfully.

### The Veterinarian's Dog

For almost ten years I regularly took long day trips so my dogs could see a veterinary ophthalmologist I'll call Martha, who solved a months-long crisis for Murphy. One day when Martha briefly left the examination room, I looked down and saw a "ghost" dog in the room, gaze locked on the door. With a sinking feeling, I realized it was Martha's aging dog, Pips, who had been seriously ill for months—and had clearly died and not moved on to what I call the proper afterlife.

When Martha rejoined us, I cringed as I saw Pips earnestly watching her. Since Martha wasn't open to my work, I had to be diplomatic (it's a chore sometimes), so I asked how Pips was.

Martha said that Pips had died. I offered condolences, the dogs got treated, and we headed back to Seattle. End of story, right? Except that Pips joined us partway home, eager to chat. She knew I had seen her and insisted that she was *not* going to move on.

"Why not?" I asked, assuming that, if the dead butt into your space, they want to talk. (I'm wiser now.)

Her answer was simple—and heartbreaking. She dearly loved Martha, knew how much Martha loved her, and was certain Martha couldn't go on if she went to the afterlife.

This is a common misconception among the dead. They are convinced that if they move on, the living won't survive. Certainly ego is involved, but so is enormous if misunderstood compassion. The dead don't want their living loved ones to grieve, so the logical solution is to stick around. Often the living refuse to let go anyway, so it can be hard for the dead to leave, even if they want to—and many do not. What neither side realizes is that moving on is the one thing the dead can and must do so both sides can heal.

I saw that with Pips as we chatted over the next few days. Most of us don't realize that our connections with our loved ones involve strong energetic, or vibrational, lines between us (in Chapter 8 I'll explain how this works). Although Pips was dead, she and Martha were still as energetically connected as if they were both alive. I explained that she and Martha could heal their grief only if she voluntarily moved on.

Pips insisted she didn't want to leave and needed to stay and watch over Martha. She also didn't want Martha to die and join her, so she fully understood her predicament. I told her I understood, but assured her that once she moved on and rested up, she would be able to visit while also healing and continuing her soul growth, which would help both of them. Pips slowly began to get the point.

By this time in my work I was realizing that my dad worked with the dead, so I asked him to go and get Martha's mother, Genevieve, who had died about ten years earlier. Since Pips was originally her dog, I hoped she could help. When Pips saw her standing beside my dad, she immediately perked up.

I told Pips it was okay to move to the grassy area where my dad and Genevieve were. Pips hesitated, asking again if I was sure she could still watch over Martha. I said yes as Genevieve and Dad waved and urged Pips to join them.

Pips slowly moved to stand at the border to my dad's way station, what I now call the Doorway Between Dimensions. She gingerly reached out with one paw and touched the grass on the Other Side. "It's really grass!" she exclaimed, and just like that, she was ready to move on.

She quickly glanced back at me: "Will you say goodbye for me? Tell her I'm okay?" I smiled and said I would, and she raced to Genevieve and leaped into her arms, yelling, "Thank you! Thank you!"

As soon as Pips moved on, I felt the dense energy that she'd carried shift and become lighter, and knew it would now be easier for both of them. Sadly, I tried to tell Martha the story, but she wouldn't hear it. It was a lesson in doing what you can.

**The Point:** When the living and the dead cling too tightly to each other, neither can fully heal. Once the dead have safely moved on to a way station or beyond, it is much easier energetically and emotionally for both sides to move on, and even to stay in touch, if they'd like.

After these experiences my dad started showing up in mediumship sessions, but I didn't think too much about why until I teamed up with him to help him with the dead. Since my dad is central to my work, let me introduce you to my parents—who they were, what they're up to in the afterlife, and why.

CHAPTER 3

# Alive, Then Dead: What My Parents Did

## The Lives They Lived

My dad, Ray J. Fritz, was seventy-two when he died on June 30, 1994, crippled by rheumatoid arthritis and a failing heart. He'd worked nonstop from age nine until he hit sixty and a crippling heart attack forced him out of his small-town pharmacy business. At sixty-eight, my mom, Rosemarie, had never been alone in her life. Depressed and dying of heart disease, she huddled in her ratty bathrobe with the blinds drawn, robotically playing solitaire until I told her to go have fun already. That's how she keeled over at a slot machine in Reno, ten months after Dad.

My dad was ready. My mom was not. I know that to them, at least, the biggest thing they had in common was their broken hearts. Literally and cosmically they never recovered from the early death of my brother Randy. In all honesty, they never really tried, despite their Catholic faith, Depression-era toughness, and two shell-shocked surviving children.

What goes on at the soul level? What do we hide, even from ourselves? What do we learn from that, even if we can't see it until we're dead? And then—yes, *then*—what do we do about it?

It's intriguing, in a book about the dead, to be able to examine two lives, one lived like anyone else's in all its idiosyncrasies and human kinks, and one freely chosen in the afterlife, with its own unique twists. What better way to change our thinking about how we live our lives and deaths than a true story about life and what came next? Or two stories—how my parents lived, died, and chose again?

My dad, Ray, and my mom, Rosemarie, raised my brothers and me in a small farming community in Oregon that barely hit 3,000 by the time I escaped to college.

My parents grew up in small-town North Dakota in a generation marked by the Great Depression and World War II. Mom was only nineteen when they married, and although the war was real to her, from rationing to secretarial work, it was life-defining for my dad. After Pearl Harbor, he rushed to graduate college as a pharmacist and went off to the army, determined to survive so he could fulfill his dream of becoming a doctor.

My dad's dream died somewhere in Italy. A US Army captain, he trudged through the Italian countryside, ending up with several Purple Hearts, a Silver Star, a bad case of hepatitis, what we now call PTSD, and a lifelong hatred of guns and camping. Released from the army, he arrived home late one day, fell into bed exhausted and malnourished, and was rousted up at the crack of dawn to get a job.

After the war, his hands shook too much to make it in medical school, so he fell back on his pharmacy training. When I was a year old, he bought a small pharmacy in Oregon and settled down to raise an idyllic family—two sons sandwiching a daughter.

Although my dad is memorable for many things, two from my early childhood stick out. The first is that he never really left World War II behind, because it never really left him. From screaming nightmares to the shrapnel that oozed from his body until the day he died, my dad's wartime experiences hurt him profoundly. Nevertheless this deeply empathetic man was proud of his service and died believing in the military.

The second memorable thing was the phone ringing in the middle of the night when the local hospital needed a lifesaving prescription filled. No matter the hour or weather, my dad would wearily get up and take care of it. His business was a healing mission.

He was also an astute businessman. His pharmacy, Ray's Drug, included a gift shop that thrived with his uncanny ability to know a year ahead of time what people would buy and have it waiting for them. He was also a tough but fair boss. I clerked for him from the seventh grade through college, and although I have a graduate business degree from a top university, I learned the important things in business from him.

Between his business and family lives, my dad didn't have the luxury to retreat. Being a pharmacist is a hard job, especially in a small town, and harder yet when you're an unshielded empath like my dad (because who understood energy back then?). Dad would come home drained and recuperate Sundays in the summer when we all went fishing.

My dad's heart went deep: he was always helping people. It saddened me that he needed a tough, sometimes gruff exterior to deal with needy sick people and get through the long, hard days. Even now, I wonder if anyone besides me understood and cherished his soft, loving heart.

I was there: I saw it. Like the time a young man came in for a prescription for his wife. As he shakily blinked back tears, I realized she was likely dying. My dad filled the prescription, carefully tucked it in a bag, and gravely walked over to him. As the man pulled out his wallet, my dad shook his head, handed him the bag, and said, "No, son, go home and take care of your wife."

Like all of us, my dad had his faults, but when his light shone, it lit the world. He was a strict taskmaster and yelled a lot, which was hard for me, the sensitive introvert. He expected me to be great in school, even though he disregarded me as a woman, saying more than once, "You should have been a man."

A product of his time, he believed what his religion and culture dictated—that women were inferior to men. Still, he was proud of me, even as I baffled him by rebelling against religious strictures (like females having to wear hats in church), or by preferring nature to people. Even today he still says I was a strange child, which is how a man who survived World War II and McCarthyism would describe a child who talked with land and weather systems and took crowing lessons from chickens.

My mom believed the same crap, even though it crippled both her self-confidence and the self-love she needed for soul growth. My parents swallowed their Catholic teaching and cultural dictates to the last drop, even sacrificed to send their kids to Catholic schools through college. I never understood how they did that, but they did, even when Randy happened to all of us.

## Randy

Randy was the typical older brother. Five years older, he comforted me during storms, teased me unmercifully, and, as soon as Mom drove off, dumped me outside the wrong classroom on my first day of first grade. On purpose. Yes, he was a butt. He was also an enchanter, a leader of magical journeys in the nearby forest, quick to point out foxes, deer, raccoons, quail, and pheasants. To me he was the sun, moon, stars, and everything in between.

And this I also knew, in the optimism of untried youth: Randy was invincible. Which is saying a lot, because when Catholics aren't pointing out that it's raining on your picnic, they're reminding you about dying on it. We were flat-out going to die, all of us, no exceptions.

Except, I decided, Randy. So of course he did die. Twice. Ripped away first from our weekday family life, to live with our grandparents to start Catholic high school in nearby Salem. Then, two months later, ripped away again, this time by leukemia.

I was nine then, Randy fourteen, and once he left for high school and became ill, he was home with us only for brief spells between hospitalizations. The last time I saw him, he looked up at me from his hospital bed and we reached for each other, clasping hands. As I met his intent gaze, I saw reassurance. Resignation. And, shockingly, farewell.

Randy was never told he was dying, but he knew, as I dimly knew in that moment. I still feel that our parents betrayed all of us by their silence, but to be fair, they had only a few days to absorb the news themselves, and times were different. Leukemia emotionally destroyed our family, snatched us from each other when we needed family the most.

The days after Randy's death are a pained blur. I remember staring in horror at what was left, lying white and stiff in a satin-lined coffin, at his cold, rubbery hand, which they forced me to touch, to make it real, as if my grieving heart weren't already reeling. I remember fleeing the funeral parlor, stomach lurching, body shaking. And standing prim, proper, and frozen with grief and confusion at his funeral while people vainly tried to comfort me with religion.

Randy's death shattered our family and my parents' simple belief in happily-ever-after-you-win-a-war. After I buried my mom, the Franciscan priest who was my parents' close friend for decades described them as the "most emotionally blocked" people he'd ever known. Of course they were: back then no one knew how to meet death, let alone help survivors.

What Randy left behind was an image of a beloved, virtuous son and brother, gone too soon. Years later as I began my intuitive work, I learned the shocking truth. As painful as it is, I'll continue Randy's story in Chapter 6, to illustrate how complex life and death are, and to reaffirm how love is always the answer, no matter what. No. Matter. What.

## To Michigan and Back Again

Life moved on in that way it has of shoving aside everything but the practical get-through-the-day activities. After I married, I spent ten years in Michigan, working full-time and attending graduate business school at night. During that time my dad suffered a massive heart attack and, six weeks later, developed rheumatoid arthritis. The man who was sick only a handful of times in my entire life, who cared for two sets of in-laws and siblings, was never again able to work.

When I divorced and moved back to Oregon in 1985, my treasured English cocker spaniel Maggie went with me. When I first met her, she was a five-and-a-half-month-old puppy who'd just lost her show prospects to buck teeth. Busy playing across the room when I stood to leave, she whirled, stared at me in shock—"*What, you're leaving?*"—and dashed across the room to frantically climb up my body, wrap her front legs around my neck, and plaster herself to my chest. In the shocked silence that followed, the breeder said, "If you hadn't already decided to take her, we'd insist on it now. She's clearly chosen you."

Indeed. Maggie was my soul mate making her second appearance in my life (yes, second), and from that moment we were inseparable. Of course she moved back to Oregon with me, and during the last few months of our life together, we lived with my parents.

It was an interesting time, being the adult daughter home again after a decade's absence. By then my parents were firmly settled in a remote riverfront home along the Santiam River, about twenty miles from the town I grew up in and light-years from the socializing town life Mom craved and Dad abhorred.

My mom, the fun-loving bottle-redhead, had done all the proper womanly things, from running charitable events and playing bridge to raising kids while hiding depression behind the expected façade of a compliant housewife. I would occasionally look at her and see a lonely, vulnerable person whose deep-seated need for approval warred with rampant self-doubt and unexamined insecurities.

In retirement and chronically bored, my mom polished her card-shark skills at local bars when she wasn't gambling in Reno. And, chronically worried about the stability of Detroit Dam upriver, she kept a watchful eye on rising river levels and the dam's emergency contact number in her address book under *H*, for "Detroit Dam—Help." She used it, too, every time heavy rains caused flooding. When I asked why she lived on a river, she pursed her lips in annoyance and muttered, "It's for your father."

Dad would just laugh and wander off, whistling. I don't think he ever understood her frustration. She played her subservient role well—or not, considering that, a decade before, she'd sold the family home out from under them both one Sunday afternoon when someone simply asked her to. It was a sweet deal, too, for Dad. Freed from the burden of being a small-town pharmacist, when people annoyed him and were ill besides, he now caught salmon out his back door. He settled into retirement in a pair of black horn-rimmed glasses from the fifties that we eventually buried him in and puttered around a woodsy yard packed with exotic rhododendrons, accompanied by devoted squirrels and hummingbirds.

I now realize my dad was not just an empath but an animal communicator, which I'm certain he never realized—it wouldn't have fit his carefully proscribed mindset. He also never understood having dogs in the house, and Maggie was a mystery, far removed from the outdoorsy Vizslas of my childhood. Sadly, she died six months after we moved in with my parents. Shortly afterward I left for a new life in Seattle.

Dad's retirement was twelve years of agony. Bypass surgery gave him a few more years, but his weakened heart and rheumatoid arthritis left him functionally disabled. Throughout it he rarely complained, doing his best to be a husband, father, and, finally, grandfather to my nephews. For two years before he died, Dad was a shriveled old man, frail, half blind, and groaning in pain; whenever I'd visit, I'd hold back tears and shock as he muttered about wanting to die.

Somehow, though, his frail body hung on. The last few days of his life were so bad that even home care couldn't help, and my mom admitted him to a nearby nursing facility. As his medical power of attorney, I honored his last request: he had signed a DNR, and left clear directives on withholding food and water. Hospice was in its infancy, so I was left alone to honor his wishes until, at last, a hospice team member arrived. I knew that, as a pharmacist who had studied to be a doctor, he understood what it would be like, and I was giving him what he wanted—the swiftest death possible.

Sometimes love seems impossible, when it is really the only thing left.

I was graced with the last words he ever spoke. As he drifted in and out of consciousness his last few days, he woke briefly, smiled hugely in delight at seeing me, then asked me what was going on. My brother and my mother, who always avoided tough issues, had insisted on not telling him, but in those moments I rebelled, my father's strange daughter to the end.

"You're in a nursing home, Dad," I said gently. "You're dying."

He nodded. "That's okay. I'm ready," he said, and smiled when I said I loved him. He never spoke again, dying around 2:00 p.m. on June 30, 1994.

My mom sank into depression, lost and alone for the first time in her life. I finally urged her to go on vacation, knowing there was only one place she ever wanted to go. She had her house thoroughly cleaned—"I want it clean for her," she told her weekly housekeeper, speaking of me as she foretold her own death—and took herself off to Reno, where she collapsed and died.

She knew she was dying, but I ignored her warning. She'd asked me to stay the month before as I was heading back to Seattle, saying she wasn't going to live very long. "Right," I said. "I'll see you later." I did, but not quite the way I expected. Mom died on April 26, 1995.

## My Parents' Afterlives: Their Life Reviews

Losing my dad was one of the worst experiences of my life. Like most people, it never occurred to me that I'd ever talk with him again, let alone work with him, but that changed when I started exploring intuition and energy healing with my dog Murphy in 2001.

One of the things Murphy and I shared, besides a strange funny bone, was a host of autoimmune issues, which we eventually conquered together. I explored traditional and alternative medical care and eventually discovered energy healing with spirit guides while working with a Seattle psychic, which turned my world upside down. I had a hard time making sense of an intuitive, or "spiritual," world so alien from the rigid Catholic one I'd been raised in and rejected. Fortunately (or not) I'm terminally curious.

One day the psychic called to tell me she'd been hearing a buzzing in her ear for a few hours, and when she finally checked it out, she discovered it was my dad, asking to talk with me. He had been watching me intuitively grow and learn, especially in my energy healing sessions, and figured out that if he could get the psychic's attention, he could get mine.

It had been eight years since he had died, and I'd considered him dead and gone. Who wouldn't? I didn't even understand intuition back then; all my experiences had been accidents, things that just happened. But when Dad came looking for me, I was thrilled at the chance to talk with him. He said he'd been reviewing his life with his spirit guides and needed to talk. (See, the dead do check in with us, especially when they're doing a life review.)

As we talked, Dad laughingly held up his hand, using that "phone me" gesture we use to tell our friends across the room (or dimensions, in this case) to call us. He'd been eager to talk, and his spirit guides encouraged him to figure out how to "phone home" on his end (yes, I inherited his "take charge" attitude).

Dad wanted to apologize for not being as supportive as he should have been, since he had blindly continued the tradition of viewing women as inferior to men. We reviewed past lives together as father and daughter in which he ruled with an iron hand, firmly in control, oblivious to my feelings or wishes. (More recently I've seen other past lives where we were close male friends, not family members.) While I accepted his apology, adding that I still loved him and it didn't matter, he was adamant that if he ever had a chance to be my father again, he would do a better job of it and treat me as an equal. Little did we know we'd get that chance while I was still alive.

Here's a cool fact about the dead. While reviewing his life, Dad had been considering what he could do next. He'd learned what he could from the life just ended, made amends where possible (hence our conversation), and lovingly accepted himself. Then the bonus kicked in. What was that? After they successfully finish their life reviews, the dead can *change their age*. When Dad showed up in 2001, he was no longer the withered old man who had died in a decrepit seventy-two-year-old body: he was vigorous and healthy, and had reverse-aged to his preferred ideal, a fortysomething man.

How awesome is that? And no, it doesn't mean they have bodies in the afterlife, because they don't. They do, however, have memories of bodies, and when they choose to use those memories, they can actually take that appearance. So when they see each other in the afterlife, and when we, the living, see them, how they look gives us a real good idea of where they are in the process of self-discovery and soul growth.

For example, my mom joined us in one of our conversations, but only after I asked for her to come. Dad said she was refusing to do her life review because she didn't want to examine her life, hiding from its truth just like she had when she was alive. (See how failing to love ourselves hurts us, alive and dead?) Her refusal showed: she was lackluster and hadn't changed a bit, still looking like she had when she'd died. When I asked her why she was holding back, she said she wasn't worthy.

"Of what?" I asked.

Of the intuitive work I was doing.

"But Mom," I said. "We did it together for years, remember? Talked with ghosts, saw things, knew things were happening. Don't you see that now?"

"But who was I to be able to do something like that?"

"You were somebody who could do that, like me. We all do something. That's what you could do. You did it naturally. The problem is, your parents never really loved or valued you, no matter what you did, so you always felt inadequate and unworthy. It's not true. You just needed to believe in yourself. All that stuff you believed, about women being inferior to men, it's just crap. It's not true. Quit believing it. Believe in yourself instead."

Mom and Dad looked at each other, and then she said to me, "You're the only person who ever understood me."

And that was it, Mom left. In a later conversation, Dad said that talking with us had helped her go ahead and do her life review, and she was now a healthy younger woman in the afterlife. That made my mom the first dead person my dad and I helped together. Interesting, isn't it, how love works? My mom and I never really got along, but we absolutely understood each other. It just took a conversation after death to prove it. It helps, doesn't it, to think that love is never too late?

Let me emphasize what I have learned about life reviews. If you don't do a life review with your spirit guides, you will get stuck even though you have safely transitioned to your proper afterlife. The difference is you *have* transitioned. However, you must still keep growing and learning, and that starts in earnest with a life review, when you get down to the hard but ultimately satisfying work of objectively evaluating how you lived the life just ended: what you set out to do, what worked, what didn't, why, and what it means for your soul's growth.

Without a life review you simply hang out in the afterlife, never growing or changing. You essentially "stew" in your own personal mix of inadequacies, worries, fears, and obsessions, without the one ingredient that really matters: unconditional love, that choice of acceptance and inclusion, no matter what.

Unconditional love looks at every flaw imaginable and still, no matter what, refuses to allow fear to stifle us. No matter how many times we fail because we're human, no matter how many mistakes we make, or how good or evil we are, the one thing we can and must fall back on is not setting limits on the power of love to guide, enhance, and illuminate our lives—and afterlives.

In every single lifetime, our fallback position is always choosing love over fear—love is what we are all yearning for, and fear holds us back. The problem is actually following through with it. Life reviews help us refine love for our unique situation. When my mom finally chose love, she went on to her life review and her fear took a backseat, so to speak. She was then able to both admire and learn from her life's triumphs and tragedies and courageously and lovingly choose a new adventure. As it turned out, my dad already had.

## Choosing What Comes Next: My Parents' Soul Purposes

A life review wouldn't get our souls very far if we didn't use it to choose what comes next. Life reviews are objective and clarifying: we get to see all the wonderful (and not so wonderful) aspects of our life, and how our choices were affected by our thoughts, beliefs, and the world and people around us. For example, what was really happening when we argued with or attacked everyone who questioned us, whether they were being cruel or obnoxious, or simply concerned and speaking up?

At the end of a life review we decide what to do next. What experience will allow our soul to grow in love and connection? Some souls decide to hang out for a while in the afterlife, to have adventures or explore their lessons and insights more deeply in etheric form. Some choose to reincarnate in some form, and others do not.

Although my mom became younger after her life review, she was still tortured about the lack of love from her parents in her childhood, which made her reject me because I, too, was female. In a touching ceremony similar to what I now offer clients, I gave Mom back the hurt she'd given me, and she turned around and gave it back to her parents.

As a result, we both healed that trauma, and my mom promptly reincarnated. She is now a delighted, happy, well-loved female child of a loving couple—in Ukraine. Her soul purpose: to knowingly experience self-love.

I wonder about her life and am thrilled she can now accept love and thrive in its generosity. It shows how our souls grow in different lifetimes, if we allow them to, even if we don't remember our previous lives, as few do without a formal past life regression.

My dad has given me permission to relate a conversation we had on June 11, 2014, which was my parents' wedding anniversary. Dad spoke about regret. He wondered if he had served Mom properly during their marriage. Did she not feel loved by him? What could he have done better? Why did she need to reincarnate to experience love? The conversation made me teary: we all have regrets, but this was my father, talking about my mother, and they were both gone.

"Maybe you were exactly what she needed," I said, struggling to comfort him. "That lack wasn't just that lifetime; it went way back. Maybe you were the one who cherished her enough that she could bridge that gap, to see what she was hiding from and start to heal, so she could start over again and feel cherished from the moment she was born."

My dad looked startled, as if that hadn't occurred to him. "Maybe so," he said, and smiled. I think that helped both of us. It's a reminder that we are "still human" in the afterlife. We still have hopes, concerns, regrets, and desires. Kind of cool, really.

Here's another neat thing about the afterlife. Although I know my mom has physically reincarnated on Earth, an aspect of her previous life as my mother remains in the afterlife. I know because I've asked her to show up at my dad's way station when family members have died, so she can greet them with my dad. She does, laughing and hugging them (and looking vigorous and healthy again).

So how can part of your soul remain in the afterlife and still reincarnate? I know this is shocking, but I don't know everything, only what I experience and observe. Souls are eternal, and soul aspects of each of our previous lives seem to remain present in the afterlife, perhaps like a linchpin. That means many parts of the same soul are there, just as it can incarnate in many different bodies over time. Talk about crowded!

What about population increase, from thousands of people eons ago to over seven billion today? Are new souls being created? Maybe, but I have yet to meet a "young" soul, although others claim they exist. However, souls don't always choose human bodies, they don't always reincarnate, and they can incarnate in multiple bodies simultaneously (as I'll discuss in Chapter 7). The afterlife seems to be infinite in size (it would have to be, right?), populated by many souls who've had many incarnations. Do you think they get together for a latte? Or maybe just to laugh about how much they forgot when they were in bodies, thinking that was all there was?

But back to my mom. I know my dad still talks with her in the afterlife, even though she doesn't appear to have a job like he does. I think her soul part's job is to grow and develop as she contemplates love. The few times I've seen her, she belly laughs, the deep kind of laughter that nurtures, heals, and connects. My mom is seeking love in a new body and contemplation in spirit, and deserves it.

Her struggles had a happy ending in reincarnation. However, other souls are extremely troubled, as I'll discuss in Chapter 6. Just because you make it to your proper afterlife doesn't mean it is all fun and games. Soul growth goes on forever. It's tough, and some souls struggle for eons. Others have such a great time—traveling the universe, exploring distant planets, playing in dimensions they can't experience in bodies—that I wonder why any of them choose to come back at all.

With so many choices, why did my dad decide to remain in the afterlife to run a Way Station for Dead Things on the Other Side? I'll let him explain it. The following is from a conversation that was facilitated by another psychic on December 28, 2012.

> **Me:** How did you come to run a way station?
> **Dad:** Quite by accident. I didn't really want to die, to go. So I hung out, and all these people were walking past. I started asking them where they were going and who was taking them there. Some were very distressed, so I wanted to help out somehow. I didn't know that who I was really

helping or who wanted help was me, but I wanted to help them, so I followed them. And I could see it all, and other spirits, other people, couldn't see. They were blind in that place, but I had binoculars on. I could see everything.
**Me:** Everything what?
**Dad:** All the people who were walking, where they were going, the people who were trying to help them, the people they had left on Earth, and the energy of the people reaching up for them and trying to help them. So that's how it started. And I just decided I wanted to be helpful, and people obviously needed help sometimes. That's how I've begun to do that. I don't know how much longer I will do it, but I will do it, and I am excited for the moment that we are able to see each other in this plane.
**Me:** Pretty cool!
**Dad**, laughing: Yep.

Dad had no sooner died than he noticed people wandering around in the Gray Zone (see Chapter 4). He didn't know what was going on, so he asked, and, seeing their distress, he wanted to help them—and himself. Isn't that ultimately what we're all doing, trying to save ourselves, with maybe something left over for others?

I was stunned and devastated when he said, "I didn't really want to die, to go." The man who'd been hampered by a painful, debilitated body, who deliberately refused food and water so he could die faster, didn't really want to die? I was appalled until he made it clear that, no, he did not want to live in the body he was in, but he did want to enjoy life in a healthy body. Which was impossible.

Dad knew all this before he did his life review, which helped him choose his next soul experience from broader, more complex possibilities than he had when he was alive. He turned his concern for the grieving dead into his new soul choice as a way station manager.

He also remembered that, when he was newly dead and in the Gray Zone, he could see things the other dead around him could not—energy lines connecting the living to the dead as both sides looked for each other. That was a big reason why he insisted I become a medium—and why I agreed.

I told him how much I appreciated him working with me and my clients and students.

> **Me:** I know it's helped me, when people come to talk with their dead, to ask you to go get those people and animals to talk with. It's cool.
>
> **Dad:** It makes it easier for you, because you don't have to search for them. And that's really what I saw as the need. Everybody was searching, the people on the planet were searching for them, they were searching for the doorway, searching for peace, for parts of themselves, and this way you don't have to search. I will help you.

He went on to discuss his concern for the stuck dead, which I'll discuss in Chapter 9.

So, how is he doing? A psychic I know was intrigued by his work and checked in on him. Tears deepened her voice as she told me that he is "well loved" in the afterlife, respected, appreciated, and admired for his loving service. It delighted me to know that the generous heart I knew so well, the devoted, sensitive, private pharmacist, is recognized and loved now for his work. He deserves it.

It took a while for us (okay, for me) to realize that we could partner to work with the dead. As he said, I don't have to search for the dead: all I have to do is ask him to go find them and bring them back to talk with me and my clients. This gives me more time to facilitate deeper conversations, which he knew, from his observations and his own search for me, could help the living and the dead get closure.

Neither of us knows how long our partnership will last. I laugh and tease him that I keep making up things for him to do, because I'm selfish and don't want to lose that fun, deeply moving partnership with him until I die and can be with him again. He teases me back, adding odd touches to our mediumship sessions "to keep me interested." He partners with me in my private and public work to make the reality of death clear to us, who wonder about and grieve for our lost beloveds, and, of course, can't help worrying about what comes next for us.

Think that's knock-your-socks-off wonderful? Well, there's icing on the metaphysical cake, and that's the afterlife and soul purpose of my beloved dog Maggie, who died on January 6, 1986.

A soul like any other, Maggie also had to choose what she would do next. Maggie's soul is the most advanced, complex soul I know. She weaves in and around my life, which I discuss in Chapter 7, when I explore her next incarnations as my soul mate dogs. However, remember how the memories of a soul's incarnation remain as a soul element in the afterlife?

While Maggie was still with my family group in the afterlife, my dad learned to cherish her, and when he decided to run a way station, Maggie went with him to help. Although I see her here with me on occasion, to play, check in, comfort me when it's time for a family member to leave, or find another way to reincarnate with me (that rascal), the soul element who was Maggie now works with my dad and the dead.

Her job? She escorts deceased animals and people to my dad's way station, greets the newly arrived, and comforts those who are still uncertain about moving on, especially children. When she was alive, I used to think she was hopelessly stupid, but she wasn't the one with the problem. Maggie always knew exactly what she was doing and still does. I am thrilled and touched that my dad, who adored wild animals and had a soft spot for my dog even as he pondered my devotion to her, would not just seek her out in the afterlife, to take care of her for me, but then readily partner with her to help the dead on their way to new adventures. The circle of life, indeed.

I don't know what their souls' futures will be, or how long they will work together to help the dead claim healthy, productive afterlives. It's enough for me that they love what they are doing and share it with me.

Together, my dad and I are working to help people understand that there is no reason to fear death, because it is simply another, different part of life. Together, we have Maggie as a joyful companion, comfort, and guide. Together, we help the living understand what dying is really like and the stuck dead release their fear, choose love, and make it to their proper afterlives.

We are helping every soul we can reach absolutely know this central truth: death is the next step on our journey, and love is the road we all walk, together.

Stories like my parents' help us understand how people meet and master challenges. Now it's time to learn how the afterlife works, starting with what happens immediately after we die.

CHAPTER 4

# The Gray Zone: Suddenly (or Not) You're Dead

What happens when you die?

No matter *how* you die, the result is the same. Bluntly, you wake up dead in the place I call the Gray Zone.

That you wake up dead isn't a bad joke: it's the plain, simple truth. Believing it matters, because death is a huge transition. Have you ever awakened from a nightmare, or in a hotel or hospital room, and wondered where you were? Even though you wake up in the same world, it can be confusing and disorienting until the world makes sense again. Waking up dead is harder. The world we lived in isn't there anymore. The basic parameters of life are gone.

So, you die and wake up dead. The problem is …

Our culture and our programming as organic beings have taught us that death is something to avoid at all costs. After all, nothing in nature is inherently suicidal, or life itself would be a paradox, right? Death, then, is something to fight, to resist and fear, because it ends everything we physically see around us and know is true. It is particularly scary for the unprepared—those who refused to think about death while they were alive—because they have nothing to fall back on.

Since our hearts and brains are attuned to the world we

consciously know and struggle to survive in, its sudden absence is disorienting, if not downright terrifying. This is when the newly dead can panic: *I didn't make it.* Except, of course, they've forgotten (or never knew) that the things that really count *have* survived death: their soul, consciousness, and free will. They've simply left their bodies behind and arrived in another place. However, death is a completely new environment: even if we're prepared, we need our wits about us to successfully navigate it and the confusion, doubt, and hesitation that can cloud our thinking. Add panic to the mix and everything gets worse.

The problem, then, isn't that death is inevitable, but that everything about life rejects death, because it is the end of our physical reality. The solution? We need to counterprogram ourselves to recognize that death is part of life—the end of one form of existence and the beginning of another. Not only is that true, but it can keep us from panicking when we wake up dead. Because we all will.

On a spiritual or metaphysical level, there are many things people can do to prepare themselves for death, but the most important is to be practical. That means thinking ahead. While you're alive, drill into your head, and especially your soul, that death is simply a new set of experiences that lead us to more experiences—as my dad says, amazing things that are possible only after you've let go of your body.

Remember this: if you suddenly wake up and things are significantly different from the last thing you remembered, you're probably dead. You absolutely, positively, must remember this, because not much will happen until you realize you're dead. When you do, you have important decisions to make, choices that determine whether you move on to your proper afterlife or get stuck. The confusion and disorientation that often accompany waking up dead can muddle the decision process.

So back to the question, what happens when you die?

Every dead person I've ever discussed this with says they woke up in a different place unlike anything they ever saw when they were alive, and certainly far different from the last thing they remember seeing. It often appears as a gray or hazy place, almost foggy, which is why I call it the Gray Zone. Naturally, the dead wonder what's going on.

Sometimes they're completely alone, which is, to put it mildly, upsetting. Sometimes they are accompanied by their spirit guides, or spiritual team. Unfortunately, the dead don't always recognize their spirit guides, because that's something else they didn't know about when they were alive. Nevertheless, they will often quickly come to accept, trust, and listen to them. It's as if their soul, which has been through this many times before, recognizes spirit guides, even if consciousness from the life just ended does not.

Sometimes, though, spirit guides take a backseat at this stage. I don't know if it is the dead's confusion or the cultural mindset they died with, or what, but they sometimes neither recognize nor accept help from their spiritual team. Hard to blame the dead, though, right? After all, you wake up in an unfamiliar place and strange beings are trying to chat with you. I'm sure if that were me going ignorantly into death (and I know it was, in many previous lives), I'd flip out.

But there's a scarier reason why spirit guides may not be there: as I pointed out earlier, they can and do mess up just like we all do, so they sometimes lose their people after death and scramble around looking for them. This means that the dead sometimes wander the Gray Zone by themselves until their guides catch up. I know this isn't comforting information, but it's true. It should remind us that we are each in charge of our own life and death, and that we should be grateful for help but not depend on it.

The newly dead also often notice other dead people wandering around. Some are upset, others confident, and all are searching, trying to decide what to do next.

Sometimes—in fact, often—people immediately realize they're dead. They're not a bit fazed by discovering there are no harps or angelic choirs waiting for them, let alone pearly gates, and they act. Okay, they may be startled to find out being dead doesn't look like what they were expecting, but they're quick on the uptake.

More than likely they're not that thrilled about being dead—biology is destiny, right, and we're back to that "programmed to survive" bit—but they're resigned and curious about what comes next. Maybe even excited. And they act. For a while they may walk around in this strange in-between state they find themselves in, but they're very clear about what it is. They know they need to be looking for something, and assume they'll know it when they see it—and they do. (More on that in a bit.) These dead are savvy and easily make it to their proper afterlives.

Other newly dead notice the ones who seem to know what to do and who march right on … somewhere. However, they might not know what to do, or be ready to accept being dead and move on, or even get what made others so confident, so they hang around and check things out. Eventually they figure it out and move on to their proper afterlives.

Others wake up and know they're dead and have a decision to make. However, they may be confused or disoriented because it doesn't look like what they were expecting, or they are quite aware of the mistakes they made while they were alive and fear punishment, or their deaths might have been unexpected or even violent. At this point, many realize they really didn't know what to expect, because religion and culture were fuzzy on the details. Others wake up dead and aren't exactly sure what's going on, where they are, or even that they are dead.

These people do not know what to do. They often notice other people who are also searching, including the ones who seem to know what's going on, but it doesn't matter—they don't know what's happening and aren't ready for anything, so they avoid making a decision. Or they hesitate, doubt sets in, and they still don't decide. Unfortunately, not making a decision is also a choice, and it can be a bad one. All of these people get stuck, and they go somewhere else entirely. More on that in a bit, too.

The good news is that most of the newly dead eventually get oriented well enough to understand that they've died. If they don't, somebody has to tell them: either their spirit guides, if the dead accept them, or a medium like me. Or—and this is important, so I will emphasize it a lot—any loved one who is still alive can simply talk to their dead and urge them to move on, whether or not they think the dead can hear them, because they can and do. Please, please understand this. No matter how prepared you think your loved ones are, leap right in after you know they've died and tell them they are dead. I guarantee it will help.

## One More Thing

Please understand: the Gray Zone is not a bad place, and no one should be afraid of it. The dead are afraid of it only because they didn't know what the afterlife was really going to be like and they were expecting something else (and possibly unpleasant). In no way does the Gray Zone equate to what some people call purgatory or limbo or whatever. It is *not* a punishment zone or a waiting place where people have to somehow redeem themselves.

Yes, people wander the Gray Zone and may get stuck because they don't make a decision. However, making a decision can take time for a very good reason: the Gray Zone is a necessary stopping point between life and the afterlife. It is where souls first go after death, so the dead have to make two decisions: *what* to do next, as I've shown above, and *when* to do it.

Let me emphasize. Yes, the newly dead have to get up and get moving, to make a decision about whether they'll move on to their proper afterlives. Or not. But they also have to decide when to move on, and just like everything in the afterlife, there's no judgment in that. It's a matter of energy density.

The newly dead are still connected to the denser energies we associate with being in physical bodies. It takes a while for those energies to release or "slough off" so the dead can more easily adjust to the etheric, or lighter, energies that are on the Other Side and that they usually first experience at a way station like my dad's.

I discovered this the hard way, which happens when I try to solve a problem and miss a step. I call this missed step "the day I broke the afterlife." (Oops.)

It was in late 2015, and I hadn't facilitated a mass crossing in months (an event in which my team and I help thousands of the stuck dead move on at once). My dad had been urging me to get back to work after a severe injury, so my friend Jody, my dad, and a number of his fellow way station managers joined me as I invited a huge number of the stuck dead to move on. As in thousands.

I asked the stuck dead, "Who wants to move on to the afterlife?"

Of course, everyone wants to, so a tsunami of souls flooded the way stations, overwhelming my dad and his friends. And then the afterlife "broke."

The problem? Most of these souls hadn't sloughed off their denser Earth energies, so they were still upset, uncertain, uncomfortable, and just plain too dense for the way stations. The managers, including my dad, promptly shut down their stations to deal with them. For weeks no one would talk with me, even my dad—they couldn't, because they were dealing with an emergency I had accidentally created. (Full disclosure: they were also a bit, shall we say, perturbed with me. Yes, they swear in the afterlife—nicely!) It was all sorted out eventually, and I was forgiven, but my slip-up made it that much harder for everyone.

My mistake? I failed to also ask, "Who is *ready* to move on?" Most of those souls weren't because they had not yet released their denser Earth energies.

So it doesn't always matter how long the dead are waiting in the Gray Zone. Unless they are genuinely stuck, they are waiting for the denser energies to lift. They'll know when it's time to move on because the Doorways Between Dimensions, which I discuss next, suddenly become enticing beacons.

Urge your beloveds to move on. That will keep them headed in the right direction, even as they wait. But also remind them they'll know *when* they're ready—and then they'll go. Unless, of course, they are truly stuck.

## The Doorways Between Dimensions

As the newly dead wander around trying to figure things out, they see round colored circles I call the Doorways Between Dimensions. I call them doorways to make it clear that they are transition points between one place and another: doorways are where we enter or exit rooms, like cave openings were for our ancestors. Here they are the points where the dead leave the Gray Zone for their proper afterlives.

Each doorway is a different color: red, green, yellow, blue, purple—every color possible. There's also more than one doorway of each color, that is, many red ones, blue ones, and so on.

The dead understand that the doorways have something to do with being dead. Most of the dead are startled, because they didn't expect to see colored doorways in the afterlife, so they will sometimes ignore them. They do notice, however, that some of the doorways are attractive, and consider walking through them. Why? The colors are attractants, like flowers to bees or honey to bears. My dad says they are like highway signs—the afterlife's beacon, signaling an exit. Cool, huh? When you're dead and see an attractive doorway, go for it, it's yours! Consider it the afterlife's cheat sheet.

The confident dead get that. They see a colored doorway that intrigues and attracts them. For example, they like the blue doorways, and the fortieth blue doorway is the most appealing. They know they need to walk through that particular doorway to get to the next phase of being dead, so they do. Presto! They've arrived at a Way Station for Dead Things on the Other Side.

Some don't see the doorways, or ignore them, or are afraid of them, or just don't know what to do about them. All of these dead get stuck.

I first noticed the doorways when my dad made it clear that he couldn't leave his way station and go into the Gray Zone because it and the afterlife are two different places, almost like life and death are. The doorways are also one-way, meaning that once you go into the real afterlife, the one where your soul continues its adventures, you never go back into the Gray Zone. That's one reason why my dad wanted me to help the stuck dead: I can work with them more easily than he can, partly because they are still more familiar with life in a body.

## The Warehouses

After the dead move on to their proper afterlives by walking through a Doorway Between Dimensions, the doorway is sealed—and stays sealed until another dead person chooses that doorway and walks through it.

When the dead *don't* walk through a doorway, they eventually end up in big waiting areas I call Warehouses. Why? Because they didn't know what to do and hesitated too long (or, yes, they're waiting for their denser energies to lift).

The Warehouses take different forms that all involve waiting. Sometimes the dead are lying down in long rows, wrapped up like mummies, refusing to open their eyes and look around. Sometimes they're standing, packed together in rooms. Sometimes the Warehouses are open spaces: I usually meet the dead wandering all alone, lost but moving and looking, but others wander in groups. They're often unaware of each other, but even if they know they're not alone, they understand that no one around them knows what to do, so time passes and they wait. And wait.

Most likely they have seen Doorways Between Dimensions, but for one reason or another they don't choose one to walk through. So they wander, and wander, and eventually give up and end up in a Warehouse. It's hard to blame them, but the part of me that wants them safely moved on does anyway. They're suddenly in a place that doesn't look anything like what they were told the afterlife looked like, and the alternatives are too scary (or depressing) to imagine.

Actually, this is pretty smart, if sad. Since being dead doesn't look like what they were expecting, they think they either ended up in a bad place or one wrong step will send them to one, so common sense would make them stay put, and they do.

Unfortunately, being newly dead is really *not* the time to hesitate, because hesitation compounds doubt, and that means the dead can get stuck. They will stay stuck until their spirit guides help, they get brave and risk moving on their own or go looking for help, or someone like me (or a savvy loved one) talks with them and helps them through it.

However, it isn't just latent common sense that makes the dead hesitate. Fear is the major roadblock for all of us, alive or dead. We fear losing the loved ones we left behind—we may even resist being dead—and believe the only way we can stay with them is by refusing to move on. The truth is, it's actually easier for the dead to connect with their loved ones *after* they move on because they are healing, but it can be very hard to let go.

We also fear punishment for things we did that we believe were wrong or even evil. We fear we aren't good enough for a glorious afterlife. We fear what culture and religion told us to expect. We fear because, deep down, we have not chosen love as our guiding principle.

It is critically important to understand fear. One of the few things with which I agree with spiritual practitioners of any faith or mindset is that there are only two choices in the world—fear and love. Choosing love—unconditional love—doesn't make us perfect or free us from grief or worry or doubt, because we're human and those issues come with the territory. However, choosing love reminds us that we can forgive ourselves for our shortcomings and refuse to let them limit us, because we are always and forever worthy of being loved. Choosing love moves us beyond fear.

The stuck dead have let fear dominate them. They wake up in the Gray Zone just as confused and disoriented as those who eventually move on to their proper afterlives. The difference is that they allow fear, which feeds limitations, to stop their forward momentum. Until they defeat fear by choosing unconditional love, they will stay stuck in the Gray Zone.

People, understand this: as the stuck dead wait, eons can go by in linear time as we know it—centuries when they could be having new soul experiences. That's tragic. It's not what souls are all about.

Then, too, sometimes the dead are not so much stuck as deliberately waiting, however misguided that may be. Why?

Families may wait for each other because they think that's the only way they can be together in the afterlife. Soldiers often wait for their buddies to join them or their bodies to be recovered. These dead can end up stuck and miss each other entirely.

Sometimes the stuck dead remember places they loved or lived in while they were alive, or places they died in, and they decide to go back to them. Although they are technically still in a Warehouse in the Gray Zone, they also inhabit those places they knew. These people become what we call ghosts, and we consider the places they inhabit "haunted." Because we, the living, tend to associate ghosts with malevolent or troubled spirits, we are often afraid of them and won't talk with or help them, so they stay stuck.

Ghosts are endlessly fascinating to ghost hunters or paranormal explorers, who try to record their images and voices, but don't help them move on. To me that's cruel. I can excuse it only by assuming that these researchers think they are recording remnants or time loops, not real souls.

My experience is different: ghosts are the stuck dead. Some know they're dead and aren't interested in moving on (these potential troublemakers are the random dead, explained in Chapter 6). However, most of them are looking for help, and many of the rest can often easily be persuaded to go. They're lucky to meet people like me who can talk with and help them. Fortunately there are a lot of us.

When I meet the stuck dead, I tell them the truth: they are dead; heaven, hell, purgatory, limbo, all of the places their culture told them to expect do not exist; and a new life awaits them as soon as they walk through a Doorway Between Dimensions and into a way station. I point to the doorway to my dad's way station and ask them if they see my dad standing there (they always do—he's waving to help us all out). I assure them that all they have to do to move on is walk through the doorway and my dad will take care of them. It always works.

## How Lives Play Out

Did that read a bit lecture-y? Let's look at the process using several fictional examples to give a broad overview, not scare anyone, and have some fun with an admittedly difficult subject.

The big day has arrived ...

Jim led an exemplary life. He bought a purebred dog and made the kids take care of it, never swore but wanted to three times (when he was seriously provoked), regularly volunteered for park cleanup projects, had 2.5 kids (the half was a mail order monthly payment to an orphanage in Sri Lanka, Africa, somewhere, his wife took care of it), never ate red meat except on sales trips, and occasionally exercised. His house was as spotless as his soul because that was his wife's job. His job was to earn the money to pay for things, and he did that. He got religion and expected to be saved and go to heaven.

Sarah was a thorough reprobate. She dissed her parents, Democrats, and vegetables. She even kicked the dog. Her floor was never, ever clean enough to eat off of. She quit religion because god was a guy, and life was too full and exciting to bother thinking about what comes next anyway. Besides, when you're dead, you're dead, and that's the end, folks, really.

Louise walked the straight and narrow her entire life. She did well in her nice, safe government job, attended every metaphysical workshop she could, was curious about crystals and chakras, and endlessly wailed about figuring out what she was really supposed to be doing with her life. She ate out a lot to avoid messing up the kitchen. Louise was sure that quantum physics was the new religion, but she could never define it, which didn't bother her one bit, because the world was an illusion, except for chocolate.

And then what? Like I said, the big day has arrived. Jim, Sarah, and Louise all died. How? At seventy Jim had a massive heart attack coming home from church. Sarah died in her sleep at forty-eight, a week before her fifteenth triathlon. At sixty, Louise got hit in a crosswalk by a drunk driver twenty-four hours before her early retirement kicked in.

Here's what happened next. All three of them woke up dead, suddenly coming to in a gray, foggy place. They were all alone, confused, and a bit freaked out: nothing like that had ever happened before. So now what?

Standing still wasn't helping, so they decided to walk around. That's when they began noticing other people wandering around like they were. Some of the people were very distressed and were crying, or angry, or both. Some weren't moving at all, and were huddled together as if scared. Others were merely observing, curious. Still others were walking confidently to colored doorways, striding right through them, and disappearing.

Jim noticed two people standing next to him, a man and a woman who both looked a bit, well, wispy. "Ghosts?" he wondered aloud.

"Your spiritual team," the man said.

"Guardian angels?" Jim asked.

"Good enough," the woman said, adding, "Jim, you're dead."

Jim was shocked. "No way. This isn't what it's supposed to look like." Then he stopped and swallowed hard, very worried. "Goddamn it, I'm in hell!" and then he gulped. Why had he waited until he was dead to swear? He thought he'd lived a good life, but he must not have, because he was scared and hurting. Wait, this place wasn't that horrible; he must be in purgatory! Swearing had done it. Swearing after he died—how dumb was that?

"So how long is my penance?" he asked his spirit guides.

Jim's guides frowned and shook their heads. "It's nothing

like that," one of them assured him. "Which colored doorway would you like?"

Jim got mad. "This isn't a game show! I want to go to heaven!"

"Choose a door," the guide said. "We'll go with you and help you review your life so you can decide what to do next."

Jim was rattled and annoyed: these ghosts sounded like old hippies. He turned his back and walked off. He wouldn't look at the doorways, but secretly wanted to. Jim ended up in a Warehouse, fuming, until one day, about twenty-three years later as the living count time, his wife suddenly showed up and frowned at him, perturbed. He perked up, and she smiled; he always acted tough, but she was the real family dynamo. As he walked over to her, teary-eyed, she took his hand and pointed to a colored doorway.

"How about that one?" she asked.

He agreed. Together, they walked through a doorway and ended up in a way station. After they rested up, they each went off with their separate spirit guides, reviewed their lives, and chose their next adventure. Jim's wife reincarnated and became a peace activist in the Middle East, and Jim came back as her cat.

Sarah, now, she of course had a different experience, because that was what her life was all about. She was quick to figure out that being dead wasn't what she'd been told, which made her feel quite smug. She was, however, less pleased to find out that two of her three spirit guides were men. She just couldn't seem to get away from them.

"We all have masculine and feminine qualities," her female spirit guide said.

Sarah wasn't sure about that, but this was a woman talking, so she decided to think about it for a while. She hung out in the Gray Zone, studying and evaluating people. At one point she realized she kinda sorta wanted to help the ones who seemed to be grieving and upset, even though she thought they were seriously shortsighted.

"Take the long view," she snapped at one, and then decided that was mean, but blowing off steam felt good.

That was when she noticed an aquamarine doorway that she couldn't resist. She walked through it and ended up in a way station run by a woman, which wasn't as big a relief as she expected, because by then she understood that what mattered was who you were, not what you were.

After reviewing her life, Sarah realized she had been a rebel for no good reason and wanted a completely different experience, one where she could sit and watch the world grow and change around her, and actually participate in creating new life. Sarah was reborn—as a volcano emerging from the Java Sea near Indonesia. Why? Because everything is alive, all souls are equal, and a volcano was the longest view she could think of and still physically reincarnate.

Louise was downright mad about being dead before she got even one day to enjoy her retirement. It took her a while to get over that. Eventually she laughed out loud when she thought about the absurdity of failing to look both ways when crossing the street, even in a crosswalk, because that was the only time she'd ever been impractical, and look what it got her—dead. However, she remembered how neat it had felt to walk around with her head in the clouds, brain almost on autopilot, even if it had gotten her killed. She loved to think about things, but she just didn't know what to think or, clearly, when. Louise spent a long time in a Warehouse until she decided that thinking wasn't as important as doing. That was when she realized that she could see and talk with people who weren't dead.

One of them, a no-nonsense woman who said she was in Seattle, pointed out the doorway to something she called a Way Station for Dead Things on the Other Side, insisting on the outlandish story that the man standing there was her father. Louise said that didn't fit quantum theory. The man in the doorway laughed out loud, saying, "Lady, don't get my daughter started."

Louise was so taken with his sense of humor and the woman's calm assurance that she decided it was time to have a real adventure. She walked through the doorway and ended up at the way station run by Ray J. Fritz. Eventually the animals there, the crops to raise, the recuperating dead people, the Sasquatches and aliens wandering around, and the constant stream of dragons dropping in for tea—especially the dragons, who knew they were real, and why oolong, not Earl Grey?—all convinced her that it was time to move on.

Louise went off with her spirit guides to review her life and pick something new. She ended up deciding to reincarnate as a human female with the goal of teaching philosophy to high school students in Missouri, but she also wanted to play and explore, so whatever she really ends up doing, she's determined to make it fun. It remains to be seen what Louise will do, because right now she's a baby, with a brand new life, death, and afterlife ahead of her—and free will, which means she can always change her mind.

Now that we know what happens when we die, and what we need to do to get to our proper afterlives, it's time to look at what happens when we get there and explore the Way Stations for Dead Things on the Other Side. But first, a healing story.

A HEALING STORY

# Unexpected Healing

Star and Ed came for a session to help deepen their spiritual life. Star is one of those women who makes you laugh because of her exuberant joy and cheerful, magnetic personality. Despite that, I saw pain lurking in her eyes, and wondered what our session would reveal. Ed was a big man, gentle and curious, but reserved.

They wanted a deeper spiritual life, but were preoccupied. They didn't understand why they were unable to have children, and Ed wanted to know the meaning behind his sudden illness. I invited their spirit guides to join us.

"In my opinion, there is no spiritual meaning behind an illness," I said. "Something happened to you, so let's explore it. Your spiritual team is saying they are proud of who and what you are, Ed, and don't think of your illness as a punishment but as an opportunity to take the time to dig deeper. Give yourself the chance to be the beautiful man you are and a role model for living in harmony and peace with someone else, whatever your family looks like. It's an opportunity for you two to grow closer together, intellectually and heart centered."

Star and Ed weren't there for a mediumship session, so I was surprised when my dad suddenly popped in and joined the conversation. While that usually meant he knew a stuck dead person needed help, he started talking about their spiritual journey.

"My dad is here and he says you need faith and don't have it. Love is what matters. When you let your heart open wide enough to let love in, nothing else matters."

I turned to Star. "Your guides are saying that you don't have to physically be a mother to show that love in the world. They know that hurts to hear."

"I believe it—it's the truth," Star said as tears shimmered in her eyes. "I know it's what's in my heart. It's hard."

I asked their spiritual teams to slow down, they were talking too fast. "I'm hearing as fast as I can!" Star and Ed exchanged amused looks, chuckling.

"They're saying to feel the deep connection you have. You two are just glowing—so much farther ahead than others. Can you share what matters to you? Yes, go out and adopt twenty-five kids. Seize the opportunity right now to be the couple who is creating something new. You're saying, 'Why did this happen? Why are we not having children? Why are you sick?' Instead, change it, say, 'What can I do and what will I do?' Feel fertility around you, fertility to create new ways of expressing yourselves and new things in the world."

Star and Ed nodded solemnly, and reached for each other's hand.

"Think of this as a nest of creation," I said. "Put into that nest whatever you want. Model what love really is in the world. What family is. Community. You as a couple. In that space you'll find ways to identify what that means to you in a concrete sense. Adopt? Volunteer in children's groups? Other ways? There are so many opportunities. Children are one method of continuing connection in the world. But there are many ways."

Misty-eyed, Star and Ed agreed. Being childless was painful for them, even disorienting, like they were lost yet trying to find their way.

Their guides had more, and I continued. "We've come to

a crossroads on the planet, with so much hatred of different races, religions, sexes. How can you create a picture of what love is without boundaries, and how do you express that? Start right here in your family. Connect all the dots. Firm it up. Then what's next? There's no time frame or limit, but it's a warm space. I don't mean to hurt you with this image, but it's like a warm, dark potential. A womb. Warm, dark, creation. So many things can come from that. What would you like?"

They wanted children, but it wasn't happening. They also wanted to start a new business and to create spiritual rituals to enrich their life together, so we discussed what that might look like.

Then Star said Ed's brother, Junior, had died a year earlier after a long illness, and Ed was concerned about his own sudden illness. His spiritual team said it would last about six months.

Ed said his illness was similar to Junior's. "Maybe that's why I'm sick, too. We lived in a damp, moldy house as kids." He sighed. "I was really healthy, and got sick about a week and a half after the anniversary of Junior's passing."

A comment like that puts me on alert, because I am keenly aware of how things can stick to our energy field. I was listening to their spiritual teams when both Star and Ed asked if Junior had made it to the afterlife. They felt he had. That's when my dad shook his head at me. Dang, Junior was stuck!

"My dad says no, he isn't there. He's in what I call the Gray Zone, the place before the afterlife. But we can help him. Let's ask him to come in." I asked Junior to join us, then turned to Star and Ed.

"The reason you feel he moved on is that he's here with you. But he hasn't. If we helped him to, you would start to get better. This is not a judgment on him or anything else. It's just how things sometimes work."

I paused to listen to Junior.

"He wasn't willing to go and was very upset about dying. He wanted to stay, which is okay, right? He was young, but his way of staying was to attach himself to you, Ed, and that is not okay. We need to help him detach from you and move on, and take what he has brought into you with him. Does that make sense?"

Star nodded. "It totally makes sense."

Ed was struggling to take it all in. The idea that a dead person, even his brother, had somehow attached to him instead of moving to the afterlife shocked him. Of course it's shocking, but it can also sometimes explain things like sudden habit changes—or illnesses. Regardless, energy healing can boost physical healing, so I was going to help Ed energetically clear his energy system to support the medical regimen he was on. But we first had to help Junior move to the afterlife.

"So why don't you say goodbye to Junior and tell him he needs to separate from your energy field, Ed. Agreed?"

Star and Ed held hands and nodded.

Ed said, "Bye, Junior. It's time for you to go. I love you very much. You'll be okay."

Sessions like this can be hard on both sides. The living are worried about their dead and their own situation, and the dead can be confused. This is where a strong spiritual team can help.

"I'm inviting his team to help," I said, then turned to Junior. "There's no harm here, Junior. You did nothing wrong. You just didn't understand. It's okay for you to go. Everyone misses you. Everyone wishes you had not died. You see, it's not your body you're attached to, it's Ed's. It's not helping him. I know you didn't intend to, but it's contributing to his illness. He needs to be healthy and strong for the rest of his life. A long, long life."

Star and Ed fervently agreed.

"You need to let go," I told Junior, and then I got firm with him, letting my no-nonsense side kick in. "You're not actually on the Other Side. You know that, right?"

Junior stared at me, confused, as I repeated his words out loud so Ed and Star could hear. *"Well, I thought this was all there was."*

"But you saw the doorways, right?" I asked, a bit schoolmarm-y, referring to the Doorways Between Dimensions that separate the Gray Zone from the afterlife.

*"Well, yeah, but then I might have left everybody behind."*

"That's kind of the point, Junior. When you don't have a body anymore, moving on to the Other Side is how you get to see them even better and keep growing your soul."

At this point, Star and Ed were laughing. "That's just how he talked," Star said.

Ed smiled. "Yes, just like that."

I laughed. "Well, I'm just repeating what he's saying. Now, Junior, you see that man standing there in that gold doorway? That's my dad, Ray. He's nodding at you."

Junior looked warily at Dad, who was giving him the same no-nonsense look I was, and then back at me.

"Yes, he's giving you a very stern look because you knew darn well you hadn't moved on," I scolded.

Junior squirmed. *"Well, but I could still see things and feel things and experience things."*

"Yes, you could, but that place you're in is a place of very dense energy. When you move on, you can still come back and visit your family, but from a place where you're completely moved on. That means your grief will lessen, and so will theirs, and you'll be able to choose something else to do."

Despite my firmness, and my dad's, Junior wasn't buying it. So I turned to Ed and Star. "He's looking at me like he doesn't believe me. Why don't you help?"

Ed and Star both urged Junior to move on, assuring him that he'd be okay and it was time to go.

Junior was looking more closely at my dad and his way station, so I seized my chance. "There are so many things you can do on the Other Side. I know you see them, that bear and deer. They work with my dad." Yes, Raymond the Bear and Ralph the Deer had joined my dad and were trying to help.

I tried to hold back my laughter as I glanced at Ed and Star. "He says, *'Why the hell is there a bear here?'*"

They burst out laughing.

I laughed, too, saying, "Well, Junior, because that's the very adventurous place we're sending you to." Then I turned to Ed and Star, who were cracking up with me. "Did he say things like that?"

They said it sounded just like him, and I laughed again. "He's saying, *'Why the hell are there bears here?'* But, Junior, there are dogs, too, and Sasquatches and aliens."

I watched as Junior started to move, and reported to Star and Ed. "And now he's getting ready to walk through the doorway to my dad and he's looking back at me. Oh, that kid had a sense of humor. He said, *'You would have to do this with some crazy lady like that.'*"

Ed and Star laughed harder, again saying that's exactly how he talked. "Fantastic!" Star exclaimed.

I continued. "He's with Dad now, and he's saying, *'That is a bear.'*" I chuckled. "Yes, it is, Junior. His name is Raymond. You're going to be okay over there. You'll heal up. Just go and rest."

I listened as Junior got very serious.

"Ed, he wants you to know he realizes that part of why he was hanging on was that he was angry. He thought people did this to him, and now he realizes it isn't true, it's just something that happened. So he'll be okay."

As we recovered from laughing, I did some energy healing with Ed while reassuring him.

"Ed, Junior wasn't trying to hurt you; he was just trying to hang on. The little extra from him is clearing out with the energy healing I'm doing. I think you'll start feeling better emotionally, if nothing else. But when there's an attachment like this, there's every possibility you'll start seeing a huge reduction in physical issues. So keep saying to yourself, 'I will work at it; I will get better from this.' You might be a little sick now from the clearing process, but don't worry about it. Just know you'll be tired, and get lots of rest."

We ended with soothing words to unwind from a raucous, emotional session.

Some months later they emailed me to say they'd taken to heart what they had learned from their spiritual team—and from Junior's reluctance to move on—and had developed a comforting, supportive spiritual practice that was enriching their life together. That's what they had come for, so I was pleased.

Ed had also switched jobs and was feeling much better, but there was an unexpected bonus. The couple that couldn't have children were stunned when Star got pregnant. They now have a healthy, happy, much cherished son. A miracle? The results of faith and belief, like my dad had urged? Star and Ed think it's a little of both.

**The Point:** Insight and healing can occur when we're ready to claim an enriched spiritual life. And if your dead show up unexpectedly, seize the chance to reach out and remind them that it's okay to move on, because love is enough.

CHAPTER 5

# *The Way Stations for Dead Things on the Other Side*

Once the dead walk through a Doorway Between Dimensions into one of the many Way Stations for Dead Things on the Other Side, they have made it to what I call their proper afterlife and their souls can continue to evolve. This means they get to live again, however they choose to, which is the point of dying in the first place.

How and why souls evolve in their proper afterlives is up to them. What matters at this point is that the dead *have* safely transitioned and it's time for them to recuperate.

Notice I didn't use the word *heaven*, because all the "places" we're used to thinking about don't exist, and thinking they do can seriously mess us up when we die. Why? Because either people are expecting some level of punishment for what they did wrong in life—who hasn't messed up somehow?—or their expectations differ so much from the reality of the afterlife that they're too shocked, confused, wary, or scared to take charge of their afterlives. The good news? What really exists is unbelievably awesome, so if you still want to call it "heaven," consider thinking of it as something closer to what I'm about to describe.

I chose the name Way Stations for Dead Things on the Other Side because of how I see the place my dad runs in the afterlife, its purpose, my stated agenda—to emphasize what really exists instead of fuzzy religious constructs—and my own goofy sense of humor, aided and abetted by my fun-loving dad. Fortunately, the other way station managers I meet haven't objected.

The name also has cultural parallels: historically a "way station" is a stopping-off place where people can relax, rest up, and get supplies. Once people left their nomadic ways behind and settled in villages, way stations helped support them on long journeys. Today there are similar places for hikers and climbers in the wilderness (and Motel 6 for the rest of us). The afterlife way stations are comfortable time-out places where the dead recuperate while they get ready to explore another soul adventure.

## How the Way Stations Work

All the way station managers I have seen stand in the doorway to their stations to greet the arriving dead. They shake each adult's hand and hold children's hands in reassurance. They prefer to talk with each new arrival, so they like the dead to show up in small groups instead of the large ones I send in mass crossings (although they happily join in on those events). My dad greets the dead by standing in his Doorway Between Dimensions with the animals who have become his helpers, including Raymond the Bear and Ralph the Deer and my dog Maggie, whose stories I've already told.

The managers then escort the dead onto the way station grounds. Each manager chooses how their station looks and where it is. My dad's is a simple log cabin in a green mountain meadow ringed in fir and pine trees. There are no other stations or towns nearby, so, although it's large and busy, it's not a place for die-hard city people. Dad walks the dead to his log cabin, where they settle in and sleep. Because of the energetic transition out of a body, the transition from life to death is exhausting even for the well-prepared soul, so rest is essential, even if they've spent a lot of time in the Gray Zone.

If you're thinking it sounds like they could also check into a ritzy hotel with concierge service, you'd be correct—for the way stations whose managers want that look. Others choose simple homes in landscapes that are like the towns and cities we live in, or even towering snow-clad mountains. One interesting thing they all have in common: the station building itself is much larger than it appears on the outside and can accommodate as many people and other beings as the manager wishes.

This is a crucial point to me that doesn't impress my dad at all. (In case you're wondering, even after death, parent-child relationships can be challenging.) I keep telling Dad that he and his fellow dead are all energy, so they don't really take up space like they would if they had bodies. Logically, then, he could easily handle the thousands of the dead I'd like to send him at once and not be crowded. However, he disagrees: he keeps the station and its setting on a smaller, more intimate scale that means the dead take up just as much space as they did when they were alive. It is, of course, his place to run, so we end up working around my limitations—and his.

Managers also choose the kind of beings they wish to serve. For example, the deceased husband of a friend who is a powerful medium is very concerned about children, and has asked her to bring children to him. My dad is unusual in that he regularly takes in the dead of my clients and friends as well as the dead from the different dimensional realms I work in, so I diplomatically call his clientele "eclectic."

All the human-oriented way stations that I work with are managed by humans who have already reviewed their previous lives with their spirit guides and chosen to run a way station as their next soul experience. Just like any soul choice, it can later change and station managers may decide to do something else, from choosing another job in the afterlife to reincarnating in another body on our planet or another (exciting, right?).

They keep their jobs as long as they want (some I know have been managers for centuries as we measure time). My dad says he will run his until he chooses something else, so he's keeping his options open. Naturally I hope he stays with it at least until I die and go there.

Some of my other family members run way stations, including my mom's mother and aunt. I've noticed that the dead beloveds of strong mediums also seem to run way stations, although the mediums themselves might not realize it. Perhaps in these families the living become mediums (professional or not) and the dead become way station managers or assistants of some kind.

Way stations for humans operate just like real life, except their interactions include talking animals, people from different time periods, and, if they're with my dad, beings from some of the multi-dimensional realms I work with, including aliens (yes, *aliens*), what we call Sasquatches (please call them the Quinnich Nation), and dragons (interdimensional visitors who can freely visit the afterlife, and no, I can't explain that). Surprised? Don't be. Remember, everything has a soul, and all souls do the same thing: grow, which includes the afterlife.

Just imagine the afterlife conversations between people from different time periods, continents ... even planets! Even though the dead don't have bodies like they did here, they eat, visit with each other, and assist with chores. I don't know how this works, only that it does. My dad keeps telling me I don't know everything.

I got real insight into life at a way station when my beloved dog Murphy died in 2012 and moved in with my dad. I watched him fuss over her, because that's his job and he wanted to take care of her for me, but also because she can still charm your socks off to get her way.

And Murphy's way made me laugh. In one conversation she said she'd learned how to be comfortable from living with me, so she got to work making Dad's way station "comfy" enough to meet her exacting standards. She was quite pleased with the meadow and forest surrounding the log cabin, and the gathering spots with picnic tables, lounge chairs, and wild spaces in the meadow. But she also prodded Dad to add more soft, grassy patches in the sun, plenty of flowers and shade trees, and pillows to lounge on.

While she was at the way station, Murphy never stopped dreaming up—and creating—things she wanted. One day, a few months after she died, I was washing asparagus for dinner when she suddenly appeared beside me and said, "Oh, I liked that."

I smiled. "Yes, you did," I said, as I noticed my dad watching us. We grinned at each other.

"That gives me an idea for Dad—no, Ray—no, Grandpa!" Murphy exclaimed enthusiastically.

Dad groaned and slapped his head while cheerfully complaining that Murphy's ideas were a lot of work. Nevertheless, they were soon growing asparagus at the way station. Again, I can report only what I know. The dead are quite busy, and as you can see, the souls that were in animal bodies are just as capable of doing things as those that were in human bodies—and do them, regardless of the astonished reaction of the deceased humans nearby. You have to laugh. What an adventure death must be for people who had no idea that beings like dragons really do exist (okay, that's most people), or what animals or other beings were really capable of, and doing, while they were here in bodies.

Dad says the weather is usually like a Pacific Northwest spring—occasionally cool, a bit rainy, and bursting with new growth, from flowers to food. Apparently seasons are optional on the Other Side, and things like growing crops are as simple as planting and harvesting, without traditional farm worries.

Play is big on the agenda: remember, my dad said the afterlife is a party. Murphy says they play all kinds of games, especially if they involve rigorous activity and lots of laughter. Yes, our dead have fun.

One major activity is sitting and visiting with the way station manager. You can imagine how busy the managers are just being with the dead as they work through their immediate issues, from regrets to happy times. This isn't a life review, which comes later. This is decompression time at a way station with a loving, wise listener.

## Way Stations in Other Cultures

I admit I'm a cultural maverick. I've learned things about the afterlife that other people don't seem to know about because I'm open-minded and nonjudgmental. Naturally I've wondered if the afterlife as I see it applies to other cultures, since until late 2015 the human dead I worked with were from Western culture and Christian denominations. Although I could work with the stuck dead from these traditions for lifetimes, I'm always eager to learn more. And, okay, I'm nosy.

Some people would consider my approach to my work a problem (my tolerant dad occasionally tops that list). For example, a few of my shamanic practitioner friends have repeatedly told me that I am "doing it wrong." That didn't just irritate and concern me—it also piqued my curiosity. If how I saw the afterlife was correct, then it should translate to other religions and cultures—or I was wrong, plain and simple, however exasperating that would be.

I had my chance to find out on the anniversary of the bombing of Hiroshima and Nagasaki in Japan in August 2015. Mass tragedies always result in stuck dead, and on that day I thought I could learn from the dead from another culture while helping them move on. So I set up a mass crossing with my mediumship partner (my very much alive human friend Jody), my dad, and his fellow way station managers.

I was surprised and thrilled when an Asian way station manager suddenly stepped forward and offered to help. Thanking him, I asked if people from Eastern traditions really had to go down to the lower world before going to the afterlife, as some shamanic practitioners insisted, or "up" to "heaven" as in the Christian tradition.

I said, "I don't see people going down or up to the afterlife. I just see them there, in front of me, and I point to my dad and other way station managers and tell them to 'go there.' It's more left or right, not down or up."

My mediumship partner agreed. To my delight, so did the Asian manager! He said he had been doing his job "since before the wall," which I interpreted as since before the Great Wall of China was built. That meant he'd been at his job for hundreds of years.

His next words saddened me. He said the Eastern cultural insistence on direction in the afterlife was so ingrained (and untrue) that many of the dead became angry, frightened, and contentious, and then got stuck. As a result, they often didn't make it directly to a way station run by someone like him. Instead, he had to visit different way stations, gather up confused Asians, and take them to his way station to recuperate. He then joined in the mass crossing, helping us move thousands of stuck dead Asians to the afterlife. That was the time when I accidentally broke the afterlife (see Chapter 4).

Although I was pleased to learn that how I saw the afterlife was correct (come on, we all want to be right sometime), and it handily demonstrated that we should all look at the afterlife as it really exists and not as religious and cultural authorities dictate, I was still sad. These stuck dead felt so betrayed by the systems they had supported when they were alive that they were severely traumatized while in the Gray Zone. I had inadvertently made it temporarily worse by helping them get to their proper afterlives before they were really ready. I was relieved when my dad and his fellow managers finally sorted it out, but it took several months, and I still wince when I think about it.

The lesson? Don't let preconceptions trip you up. If religious beliefs comfort and inspire you, great; we all need support. Just remain open to a much different reality after death. It will help. Get to a way station as soon as you're ready and you can hash it out with the manager.

## Stories About Way Station Encounters
### It's a Family Affair

When I heard that my uncle Pete abruptly died of a heart attack, I told my dad to get ready and demanded that my mom go to his way station to greet her brother-in-law. Then I went looking for him with my mediumship partner while asking Raymond the Bear and Ralph the Deer to help, since they frequently escort the dead.

We found Pete wandering in the Gray Zone, confused. I called out to him, and he peered at me, puzzled and antsy.

"Pete, you're dead," I said.

He was disoriented but acknowledged me as he glanced warily at Raymond. "What's a bear doing here?" he asked.

I explained that Raymond was a friend and that Pete shouldn't worry, his wife was being cared for by his children, and it was okay for him to go on. Once he heard that, he was ready, and I pointed out my dad waiting for him—and my mom. Even though she has already reincarnated, the part of her soul that remembered her life as my mother was there, and as Pete walked through the doorway, they all laughed, hugged, and walked back to dad's cabin, arm-in-arm.

My dad's brother-in-law, my uncle Bill, died in July 2013 after years of illness and disability. As soon as I heard he had died, I went looking for him in the Gray Zone. It had been only a few hours, so he was still figuring things out. Confused, he looked at me and said, "Robyn, this is not protocol."

I laughed and said, "When did you ever know me to follow protocol?"

He chuckled, agreeing. I told him his wife was being cared for, and then I pointed out my dad, who was waiting for him, and Bill walked straight to him. My mom was there, too, laughing and greeting him. My parents wrapped their arms around him and walked him to the cabin.

**The Point:** Don't worry about how your beloved dead will be greeted. Deceased human and animal family members can and do show up at the way stations to greet new arrivals. And even though they may not arrive at a way station where they know the station manager, the dead will still be warmly welcomed. Always.

### The Father in the Bar

A young man, Todd, wanted to talk with his deceased dad, Ben. Instead of going to get him on his own, my dad abruptly changed his game plan and took me along. In one moment I was looking at my dad at his way station, and in the next he was standing outside a run-down rural bar, grinning at me as he opened the door and a wave of stale cigarette and cigar smoke rolled over me. It was the first time I'd smelled anything on the Other Side, so I was startled—and I hate the smell of tobacco, which my dad knew.

"Whoa," I gasped, jumping back in my chair and fanning the air, as if that could clear out the smell. "Can you cut the special effects?"

My dad laughed, saying, "Just trying to keep you interested," the same line I use on him when I'm trying something new.

Inside the bar people were drinking beer and playing pool and cards. As I watched my dad walk up to a table of poker players, one of the men turned to him, a cigar hanging out of his mouth. Dad explained that his son wanted to talk with him, and invited him to join him. In the next dizzying moment both of them were back at the way station, looking at Todd and me.

Ben listened patiently as Todd explained that he was having trouble juggling his mother's demands. Ben said Todd had done enough, the mother would never stop making demands, and it was time to take care of himself. (Todd's parents had divorced years before Ben died.)

The mother's issues had been a frequent topic of conversation when Ben was alive, and now he said exactly what he'd said then. The difference? Todd already knew he wasn't missing something that would help his mother, but he got two bonuses: permission from his deceased father to take care of himself and not feel guilty about it, and a good chuckle knowing his dad continued to enjoy cigars in the afterlife.

**The Point:** The dead do still care about us. If you ask what you really need to, you might get insight into an issue.

### A Dog Switches Way Stations

My client Joan called because her beloved dog, Baby, had died after surgery to repair a shattered leg. As we made an appointment to talk with him, I said I would ask my dad to find Baby and take him back to his way station to recuperate.

I watched as Dad followed the energy lines from Joan to Baby at another way station, which looked like a Midwestern cornfield. Dad asked the manager if he could take the dog with him.

The manager was perplexed, saying, "That's not how it usually works."

Dad nodded, saying, "My daughter is talking with the dog's owner and the dog, and I help her do that."

The manager was astonished. "Your daughter can talk with us? Then I guess you should take the dog."

Dad did take Baby with him, but only because Baby agreed to go. That helped me monitor his recovery.

In our session, Joan learned that Baby was adjusting well and that he was now young, vigorous, and running through the woods at the way station with other animals. Later Baby came to me in a dream, appearing as a giant dog who hovered like an angel over Joan. He said to tell her to help shelter dogs by walking them and loving them like she had loved him, and that he would help. She cried when I gave her the message.

**The Point:** Not even death can completely sever the ties between those who love themselves, and each other, regardless.

### A New Helper Arrives

Two days after my beloved dog Murphy died, I was scheduled for public sessions at a local store in Seattle. I should have canceled: I was deeply grieving, and that morning I had a panic attack from missing Murphy, not sleeping, and worrying that I wouldn't be able to help people. Still, I honored my commitment and went.

One client, Sharon, wanted to speak with five deceased people at once. By that time I knew my dad could help me, so I asked him to bring her family and join us.

Dad had other ideas. "I'm busy taking care of Murphy. You can handle this on your own."

"But Dad," I protested. "This is a paying client! You said you'd go get people to talk with us!"

"You can handle it on your own," he said.

Well, bummer! I was wondering if a temper tantrum would work when Murphy suddenly popped in. "I can help, Mom," she said.

I stared at her, stunned. She looked great: healthy and perky, the mischievous but serious dog who'd lived her life exuberantly. There was no sign of the wasted, weak dog who had died of cancer two days earlier.

"But Murphy," I sputtered. "You just died. You're supposed to be resting up."

"I'm fine," she said calmly. "I'll help you."

And she did, bringing in all five people to talk with Sharon while they leaned down and petted Murphy. Sharon got closure with her family, and I was in awe at Murphy's skill and composure.

Afterward I was shaking: I had not expected to see Murphy so soon after her death, and while I was relieved she was well and grateful for her help, I felt clubbed by grief. As I thanked her, I saw my dad standing beside his log cabin, watching us, and suddenly understood that he'd let Murphy take over to help us both adjust to our new reality. I blinked away tears as I watched her leap into his arms and kiss him, then jump down and tear off across the meadow to play with her new friends.

**The Point:** Love finds a way.

### Harold and Sachi

I know there are many other way station managers, but I've worked directly with only a few besides my dad. One of those was Harold.

In January 2014 my dog Alki and I were badly injured, which meant we each spent a lot of time in our respective medical facilities. At one visit to his veterinarian Alki suddenly panicked, huddling near me, eyes wide, refusing to be examined. When his panic escalated, we switched rooms, and he promptly calmed down.

What had happened? Later that night Alki's Grandma Jody and I intuitively checked into that room and discovered that a large black dog had been euthanized in it a few weeks earlier. He was not only stuck in the clinic, but had been standing there yelling at Alki, "Run for it! They kill dogs here!"

Yikes! I asked the dog if his people were with him and crying when he died, and he said they were. I told him I was sorry that they hadn't explained it to him, but it had to be because he was too damaged to live, so they had helped him die to end his suffering. Once he heard that, he willingly moved on and Dad welcomed him.

Now, I don't walk around wide open to what's around me, especially in a veterinary office, where I'm focused on a client's family or my own. I told Alki's veterinarian what had really happened and suggested he tell his staff to explain to animals what is happening during euthanasia, so they wouldn't get stuck. He was perplexed and agreed that something unusual had happened, but didn't commit to anything. You do what you can, right? Then I remotely cleared his clinic to help the other stuck animals there, sending them to my dad.

Some weeks later I planned to be with my friend Mary as she euthanized her beloved cat Sachi, who had cancer. Since I was now well aware of how many stuck animals there are at veterinary clinics, my dad and I sat down together the night before and looked at the clinic. We found so many stuck dogs, cats, gerbils, and bunnies that we decided I would get there early to be physically present to move the animals to Dad's way station before he helped me with Sachi. Being physically present wasn't necessary, but I felt it offered respect and closure for the animals, and I was going to be there anyway.

The next morning I was behind schedule because of heavy rain. As I was driving, my dad suddenly started talking. "I've asked my friend Harold to step in and take all the animals at the clinic so I can just deal with Sachi," he said.

I was surprised, but agreed. Then Harold showed up and

started to talk (and talk, and jabber some more). Harold said he ran a way station and was connected to the veterinary hospital but hadn't worked there. I would've left it at that, but when I got to the clinic, Harold would not shut up. I finally had to ask the vet tech who was with Mary and Sachi if she knew of anyone currently working at the clinic who had a dead relative named Harold.

She didn't know anyone and left, saying, "I wish some of my dead would come talk with me."

Yes, bringing up Harold was inappropriate, but I knew Mary would understand—and he was on the verge of talking me to death! (Sometimes you regret the dead don't have bodies because you can't smack them.) I could also see him clear as day.

What I didn't know until later was that the vet tech had promptly told the clinic's owner, the veterinarian who was about to euthanize Sachi, about Harold. I fully expected that I would never know who Harold was, and was beginning to wonder if I was going to have to listen to him drone on until I died, too, and could get away from him, when the door opened and the veterinarian walked in. He was the spitting image of Harold.

That's when I realized my dad and Harold had set me up. They both stood there grinning at me as I asked the veterinarian if he was Harold's son or nephew. He shyly admitted that Harold was his dad, and that I was correct—he had not worked with the animals in the clinic, but had always been interested in his son's work.

After Sachi was respectfully euthanized, and I reported her safe and sound with my dad, I chatted with the veterinarian. I told him that Harold had volunteered to be there for every euthanasia to make sure that every animal would get safely to his way station. Touched, Harold's son promised that he would make sure that he at least spoke to animals in his head as he was euthanizing them, so they understood what was happening, even if their human families weren't open to it.

This was a dramatic example of my dad seeing energy lines between the living and the dead. Later Dad said that when we had looked at the clinic the night before, he had seen the energy lines between the veterinarian and his fellow way station manager Harold and seized the chance to help them connect. Harold was grateful, because he had been unable to do that on his own. All I can say is, my dad and I frequently up the ante on each other to keep things interesting—and sometimes serendipity is a real thing.

**The Point:** Just keep doing what feels like the right thing. Somehow it will help your dead—or someone else's.

There are other things about the afterlife that will make you wonder if it's like a bang-up fantasy novel, and truth is, the entire universe is really like that, as you'll see when we explore just a few of the mysteries about the afterlife.

CHAPTER 6

# More True Things About the Afterlife

Is your mind blown yet? I hope not, because there's more, starting with the road to the afterlife through the slings and arrows of plain dumb luck—and soul choice.

## Life Sucks, and Other Fun Things

Despite all the metaphysical flapdoodle out there, this is how life really goes: we're born, crap happens, fun happens, we die. That's it. What counts is what we make of it. The fun part is easy, but what happens when things go wrong, and who do they go wrong (or right) with?

## Soul Groups, Here and Hereafter

I'll explore soul groups in more depth in Chapter 7, but here's the concept. Soul groups are groups of souls who tend to reincarnate together throughout their many lifetimes and gather together between lives in the afterlife.

Yes, whether or not we recognize them, we are most likely running around right now with some of our soul group. Soul group relationships also vary, as individual members come back as family, friends, frenemies, enemies, and complete strangers who never connect. For example, your mother or sister in this lifetime might have been a man or woman in another, including a spouse or complete stranger. And, while soul group members sometimes reincarnate together as humans, they can also come back as animals (as in my lifetime) or as other beings. Got it?

The reality of soul groups can be exciting—or depressing. You may like or dislike people you meet or are related to, enjoy or groan through shared encounters and experiences, or simply not get along (it happens). But thinking about repeating those relationships for eternity is, well, delightful or horrifying, take your pick. I find it exhausting just thinking about running into the same people with the same damn problems, over and over—including myself—and then waking up dead and finding myself mashed up with the same messed-up people!

We can learn about a soul's adventures with past life and between life regression in hypnotherapy, spiritual or shamanic healing, or daily life (think, deja vu). For example, I've learned about shared lifetimes with my animal family, my dad, and friends. I know my dad and I have spent many lifetimes as father and daughter, and others as male friends raising families in the same community. It was enlightening, and it deepened our current relationship, no question, but beware. You can find meaning by exploring past life relationships with current loved ones, but it can be weird, even creepy. I'm not sure knowing your husband or wife in this lifetime was your daughter or son in a previous one is going to do anything but give you bad dreams. This can't just be my hang-up, but there you go.

Examining past lifetimes can be enlightening, and it can deepen your current relationships, but be careful about what you are doing and why. Sure, there's the weird factor, but seeing tough elements of a previous lifetime can knock you flat. Consider how you would react if you discovered you were the world's most evil person in a previous lifetime, or just that you'd done something that horrifies you now. That happened to me: while I was experiencing spontaneous past life recalls some years ago, I remembered that I had committed suicide in my last lifetime. I was so appalled it sent me into a severe downward energetic spiral, which resolved when I learned context: how previous experiences can affect soul growth now.

If you explore past lives—and it can really help, as I've seen by taking countless clients through past life regressions—remember that your current lifetime is what counts. Work with a skilled professional who can guide you and safely hold space for the journey—especially if you suspect those spaces may need to be huge. For example, I and many of my clients have had lifetimes on other planets; in my experience, most of us who were "alien" are at least vaguely aware of it. To safely explore and incorporate those lifetimes into our current lives, you need a practitioner who doesn't blink and who can safely contain multi-dimensional energy.

So what about soul group members in the afterlife? While deciding if and when they reincarnate, they will often meet and learn together—if they are on similar soul trajectories. However, those who slip off their path can be and often are separated from their soul group until they heal enough to return to it—if they do. More on that in a bit.

## Comas and Mental and Physical Impairment

Life can be very hard. There is no reason for suffering, pain, or disability—it just happens. However, we do have choices: we can make the best of a tough situation, let it destroy us, moan and groan our way through it, or … whatever. Live and learn, right?

Some situations appear to give people the opportunity to work on soul issues or to accomplish that lifetime's chosen work without having to deal with bodily issues. They include severe mental or physical disability, crippling autism, and comas, all situations where the body simply does not function in what we consider a normal way. Sometimes people plan these events before they're born, and sometimes they don't and adapt (or not) as life changes.

Of course these conditions are devastating. We struggle to accept them, but what we don't know is how the soul uses them to engage in deep soul work—something we hardly know in good times. Be aware there could be more going on than you suspect, and decide for yourself if that's comforting—or not.

As an example, my mother's aunt was in a coma for years before she died. I grieved that this woman, who had been vibrantly healthy her entire life until she suffered a massive stroke, could spend years bedridden and largely unconscious. Yet after she died, she told me she'd used that time to resolve issues with her spiritual team so she could have a jump start on soul growth in the afterlife. She now runs a way station like my dad's. You see? We just don't know.

**The Point:** Only the soul knows what it's up to. Our job is to do the best we can with what we've got, to help when we can, and to keep on learning and growing our souls. Alive and dead.

## Afterlife Adventures

My dad and the dead I've talked with (human, animal, and other) have exclaimed about the amazing things we can only do in the afterlife. As in, go anywhere we want, *anywhere*. And celebrate with soul mates.

### Afterlife Vacations

Our deceased loved ones are often busy having a bang-up great time. They travel the world, seeing the things they didn't get to when they were alive, or revisiting them. Paris. London. Africa. Hawaii—many people, including a dear friend's family, so adored Hawaii in life that they're hanging out there in their afterlives, too.

Others travel to distant planets and dimensions throughout the universe. While I've heard about this from the dead, I got a vivid firsthand glimpse on my first birthday after my dog Murphy's death, when she took me on a wild flight to alien planets, including a planet she said was "under construction." It was dark, humid, and roiling with thunderstorms—something I love, but Murphy always hated, so we were there for only a few seconds. Another stop was the Planet of Talking Daisies; it had a bright shining sun, blue sky, and green, grassy fields dotted with four-foot-tall daisies that swayed in a gentle breeze and talked with us. Silly or awesome, you decide, but I can't wait to visit it again with her after I die.

That we can take vacations after we die makes the afterlife something to look forward to—and makes us grin, thinking what our lost beloveds might be up to. They are a good reason to wish our dead bon voyage.

Which brings us to a truly magical place.

### The Interstellar Café

Want to cheer up physicists? Tell them the afterlife includes a place that exists outside of time and space even for the afterlife. I call it the Interstellar Café, and it's like a gold star awarded every single kid in grade school, because we can all win. We start our lives with goals we chose before we were born, and if we pretty much nail those goals, or at least do the best we can (including being a good citizen of the planet and living the best life possible), we get to celebrate with the meal of our choice at the Interstellar Café after we've safely moved on to the afterlife. (One dog I know chose liver and onions, giggling because he was being fussed over by a French chef.)

We can celebrate alone (there's always a friendly crowd) or with a soul mate, as if no time at all has passed between our deaths, which is what my dog Murphy and I are planning. Imagine getting to your afterlife and enjoying a celebratory meal with a long-dead beloved at the Interstellar Café—like you were never apart.

Don't you love the Interstellar Café? It's so simple and right that we can celebrate a meal with our beloveds the moment we successfully reach the afterlife. Food sustains our bodies in life, and is one of the amazing things we get to enjoy when we leave them.

## The Perils of Classical Mediumship

People work with mediums to get the closure that an objective outsider like a professional medium can facilitate. The problem is who to choose—and why.

People have been talking with the dead as long as we've been dying. However, now that we've made it a profession, people have created rules around mediumship. This raises my concern with "classical mediums" who insist theirs is the only way to connect with the dead, which is as untrue and limiting as our culture. Now, I'm all for proper training in every field, but the mediumship and intuitive arts schools I've seen tend to equate their training with spiritual or religious dogma instead of what is actually out there, leaving their students dangerously unprepared and untrained for a complex and tricky reality.

### The Random Dead and the Rules

Until my dad showed up and asked me to work with him as a medium, I just wasn't interested in working with the dead (even then, I needed convincing). I thought all mediums did was get name, rank, and serial number from the dead, and you already know all that about your dead, so what's the point? I would also never go into a room and say something like, "I am seeing the letter M. It's a man—somebody's father or uncle," and wait for a hand to go up, nor would I do that in a private session. Why? Because my time (and yours, and the dead's) is more valuable than that.

But the scarier issue is that this practice turns up the dead who have no relationship to anyone in the group and aren't seeking real connection. I learned this after attending several local mediumship practice groups where people were wide open, eager to connect, and not as discerning as they should be.

The random dead are the dead who are in the Gray Zone, quite aware of the world they've left, and not the least bit interested in moving on. They may be slightly or extremely malicious, capricious, curious, lonely, or whatever, but they all have one thing in common: they're a potentially dangerous nuisance. These people are not like the stuck dead: they are just fine with their situation and are roaming around trying to get the attention of the living for no reason except, perhaps, to mess with them for their own amusement. Even worse, some of these beings are neither human nor dead, but are various levels of mischievous, interfering, and extremely dangerous entities that most of us today neither understand nor can safely handle.

That's one reason I insist that clients tell me who they want to talk with and why. Does that open me up to criticism that I'm cheating because I'm somehow pulling information from the living about their dead? Only from the people who've made up rules other people blindly follow and are ignorant about the random dead (and creepy company)!

I started my professional intuitive practice communicating with animals, where you always ask for specifics about your animal client, so you get the right one, and not a cranky Shar-Pei in Iowa. Somehow "classical mediums" bypass that crucial step of getting up-front verification so you can get right to the discussion, which itself reveals plenty of confirming details. The emphasis on "blind" readings assumes that people are so suspicious of the mediumship process that they start it by assuming fraud. That's untrue, disrespectful to all involved, and creates a heavy energy that can block connection and healing, leaving both sides unsatisfied. So please, take all "rules" with a boulder of salt and decide if they work for or simply limit you.

I once had a client storm out of a session because I refused to play that game. Her poor husband was standing there with my dad trying to tell her how she could connect with him herself, without a medium between them, and she was refusing to hear it because "he wasn't interested in the metaphysical when he was alive." Well, guess what? Being dead can change what you're interested in. Big time.

Because this woman had decided that mediums are supposed to play the "name that hobby" game, and I wouldn't play by those rules, she decided I wasn't legitimate. Sadly, she didn't get the real message, either, which was that she had already been connecting with her deceased husband but wasn't willing to believe in herself—or him.

Isn't the "right way" to connect what works? Do you need your dead to prove themselves, or would you rather hear about what they've learned, seen, done, and thought since they died? Even get their advice, or, what can really help both sides, resolve an issue? Once I realized my dad could help me make this kind of connection with the dead, it made sense to talk with them. It can lead to real closure, which can heal grief and help both sides move on. That is, after all, the point.

**The Medium's Dad.** Once at a public event, I exchanged a short five-minute reading with a "classically trained" medium, Kathy, whose style was to sit and wait for someone to show up to talk with her. I explained how I worked and asked who she wanted to speak with.

Kathy wanted to talk with her father, Rex, so I asked my dad to go get him. I immediately saw snowcapped mountains and felt a fresh, cold mountain breeze.

"Wow," I said, shivering. "Your dad liked cold weather!"

Kathy agreed, saying that she personally hated being cold. I then asked her what she wanted to talk with Rex about. She wanted to know if she had made the right decision. Now, here's a wide-open question that can confuse the dead in nothing flat (and annoy the medium you're paying!). As Rex looked at my dad, he raised his hands in frustration and asked, "What is she talking about? When she was making out with that boy when she was sixteen, or what?"

Kathy was reluctant to say more, and we were out of time. I told her that if I heard anything else from Rex, I would let her know (sometimes I hear from the dead after sessions end). Then my dad turned to me and said, "Rex just invited me to go for a beer, and I'm a Scotch man, but I'll go enjoy myself. You girls have fun."

On the way home both men started talking to me as they toasted me from their afterlife bar. Rex said, "If she was talking about her work, tell her to balance the investigation and science with heart and feelings." I emailed that information to Kathy and she responded, saying that was exactly what she wanted to talk about and she now had an answer—which she could've had the night before if she'd been less suspicious and more open to the process.

Try being specific with a medium. The dead are not hanging around waiting for you to talk with them. The afterlife is a bustling place, they're busy—and they don't read minds. If you get hung up on "the rules," you risk losing a great connection. Find someone who has a good reputation and trust that it will work out. Granted, no one is 100 percent accurate—not a medium, physicist, or skeptic. Sometimes the dead don't come to talk. Death is a new reality, and sometimes they can't, or they're not interested, or they don't have anything to say, or they're stuck. Trust yourself, trust the medium, trust the answers you get to your specific questions, and see what happens. Life is an adventure. So is the afterlife.

**The Point:** Be specific or risk losing a great connection—your dead will appreciate it, and so will you.

## The Unrepentant Dead

We assume that all is rosy once we've successfully moved on to a way station, and so "crossed over" to what I call the proper afterlife. Sadly, that is not always true. Souls progress at different levels. Sometimes they are locked in resentment, and it takes extreme measures to help them. These are the people—the souls—I call "the unrepentant dead." If that sounds judgmental, dispassionately call them "souls that aren't interested in transforming—and don't." Always deeply troubled, they can be spiteful, nasty, and dangerous.

The unrepentant dead are fiercely angry and determined to take it out on anyone they can. What are they angry about? None of them will admit it, but like all of us, it comes down to whatever makes them refuse to love themselves, something they'd rather fuss or fume or vent about than heal. In life and death, the bottom line is always choosing self-love.

When you die, you carry your life experiences with you, sometimes for lifetimes (a reality that has skewed the notion of "karma"). Some souls spend eons in spirit unable to transform their issues into something that would help them spiritually heal and grow. These people may or may not have understood how angry they were when they were alive, or that they might have brought that toxic brew from a difficult past life. Regardless, they won't let go of it after death, no matter how much their spiritual team tries to help. While ultimately all souls want to learn to love, which results in soul growth and healing, they have to choose it, and some take a very long time.

I know shamanic practitioners and other mediums who insist this is impossible, that such souls have simply not yet moved on, and so are actually in the Gray Zone and are the stuck dead. They believe that all that is required is to ask angels, deities, and spirit guides to surround these souls with loving energy and help them transition to the Other Side, where they will continue to evolve over time.

I wish this was true, but it is not.

From talking with my dad and my spirit guides, I know there are souls who do successfully transition to the afterlife but then spend eons unable to process or transmute their anger into something that would help them grow in love. That's a nice way of saying the dead can be assholes and stay that way on purpose, no matter how much work their spirit guides are doing, or trying to do, with them. No matter how much their soul group tries to love them. No matter what. Period.

I have dealt with several of these unrepentant dead, some who were actually people I knew when they were alive, although I did not realize then how angry they were. Being dead did not improve their attitudes. Being in the afterlife didn't, either. That's why I call them the unrepentant dead.

These people are separated from their soul or family groups, as long as those groups are evolving at a higher rate. (Sadly, I can easily imagine entire soul groups that are not interested in transformation.) Their spirit guides keep them as contained as possible, although they still have free will and can and do escape these confines to harass and torment the living and the dead. The unrepentant dead are unhappy, angry, hostile, and generally unpleasant people. (So who are nice dead people? People who continually work at growing their souls: people you would generally be safe around and might even enjoy being with.)

The unrepentant dead are not being punished in their containment. They are in a healing place that I call "Sanctuary," being held lovingly and tightly to try to prevent further deterioration. However, they have to choose to heal, and to say that some of them are, at best, recalcitrant offers some hope that they will heal, grow, or do something positive besides stay angry for eternity—hope that in some cases might be misplaced.

Sometimes these unrepentant dead escape and bother the living, which has happened to several of my students and to me. They are a huge reason why I am so concerned about other mediums, and why I'm so careful about my work and what I teach, insisting that all intuitives, especially mediums, have strong safeguards and competent spirit guides on the job 24/7.

## My Own Private Unrepentant Dead

I know about the unrepentant dead because of one who has shown up repeatedly since I became a medium: my deceased brother, Randy, who died at fourteen and was the first dead person I met. I didn't understand what he was until I visited with my parents after their deaths and asked them how Randy was doing, expecting to hear about a joyful reunion.

"Better than he was when he was alive," my dad said solemnly. I was shocked, but thought he was referring to Randy's early death. The truth was crushing.

Dad explained that after they both died, he and Mom met with Randy and discovered that he had gone into his life as their son as an extremely troubled soul and was still angry, tormented, lost, bitter, and determined to not heal. As a result, he is on a different path from theirs. He is not with the family soul group, and they spend very little time with him.

It was the first inkling I'd had that Randy was not the person we'd all imagined him to be through the filter of an early traumatic death. I remember him as a playful boy who teased and played with me, and was sometimes mean, even cruel, like we can all be. None of us ever saw the darkness in his soul that leads to someone becoming an unrepentant dead. I'm not sure he was consciously aware of it, or if any of the unrepentant dead were while they were alive. All I know is they had things to work out in their lives—the soul growth that is the point of every soul choice—and they refused to. Perhaps Randy came into his life with unresolved past life issues, or maybe leukemia triggered an intense rebellion that derailed his spiritual growth. I really don't know.

I know no one in my family ever really recovered from Randy's death—that it damaged all our lives—but until I learned the truth about him, I never considered that he might have been the most damaged of all. The horror of that time is one reason I shied away from mediumship, and why, having committed to it, I am so passionate about helping the living and the dead get closure to resolve their grief—and move on.

I knew my parents expected to meet a healthy, vibrant son in "heaven." Instead, I felt their anguish at his continued turmoil. It had to be devastating to hear their own spirit guides, and Randy's, say that while he had made some progress, they should limit contact with him and leave him to his spiritual team because he needed to heal alone. Their decision to trust his team and do exactly that was incredibly gutsy and loving. He was their son and they loved him, but they understood that the only way they could help him was to let him go.

Even now, years later, it makes me ill to think of Randy's situation—and of my parents' horror. I know my dad occasionally checks in with his team, but I have had to safeguard myself and my students from him, and don't expect to ever connect with him until I'm at least in the afterlife myself.

I once had a student who called me, very excited that Randy had contacted her and wanted to talk with me. I immediately stopped her, but it was too late: Randy came roaring forward, pushing his way into our conversation, angry, vindictive, and screaming that he "should never have been born." It took all our spiritual teams to block him until he could be returned to his sanctuary. His team later apologized, saying that sometimes the unrepentant dead do manage to evade their team and rush off to torment others.

Of course I felt terrible, since I'm passionate about supporting souls yet couldn't help my own brother. His team said his healing could take centuries and he will probably not reincarnate, which is not mandatory, but here implies that some souls just can't handle being reborn. All I know for sure is that he's getting help. Several years after that shocking encounter I asked Dad if we could try to help him like we help the stuck dead. He said Randy wasn't ready, and that's where we've left it.

**The Point:** We should encourage our deceased loved ones to love themselves, but we need to leave some of them alone.

These additional elements of the afterlife prove how fascinating and complex it is, reminding us that, alive or dead, the only things that happen for a reason are our choices.

Now, one of the fascinating aspects of the afterlife is realizing that it isn't just about humans. Since everything is alive, then everything dies, which means that nonhumans have afterlives, too. For most of us, the nonhumans that matter most are our animal families, so let's find out what their afterlives are like. But first, another healing story.

A HEALING STORY

# The Persistent Dead

Tara and her husband, Derek, came to talk with Tara's dad, Thomas, who had died fifteen years earlier. They were concerned about Tara's sister, who had miscarried at seven months and was undergoing surgery at the same time as our session, and about her mother.

Tara is a smart, vibrant woman with a love for spiritual dancing. Her quiet and unassuming husband, Derek, came to support her.

Tara felt that her dad had been present with her sister as she lost her baby.

"Your dad is already here, Tara," I said. Then I laughed. "He's listening to my dad tell me about the birthday party they were having yesterday for Murphy, my dog who died in 2012. Yesterday would have been her birthday."

"Fun and games?" Tara asked, grinning.

"Yes," I said, laughing. "Oh, and your dad is like, *'Wow, this is an interesting place.'* He's looking around. My dad works with me so there are all kinds of things—aliens, Sasquatches—at his way station. A lot of times people will come in and say, 'I always knew those things existed.' There are so many strange things in the afterlife, you'll get yourself knocked flat pretty easily. Your dad is shaking his head, saying, *'I was always a practical man, and as many years in your time as I've been gone, I've really not seen this kind of thing.'*

"And my dad, he's shaking his head, waving his hands, like, no, no, not me. He's saying, *'Yes, that's my daughter. I actually didn't see those things, either, until I started working with her.'* They're having a good laugh about that."

Tara, Derek, and I cracked up at this.

"But the good news is, he's safely moved over," I told Tara. "He's showing me a real emphasis on this baby your sister lost. In his mind all the other grandchildren are fine. This is the only one who died, right? That's what he's showing me."

As Tara nodded, I said, "It was not a surprise to him. He was aware this pregnancy would not go to term. He's saying this baby wasn't born. It already had one step in the afterlife."

"Yes," Tara said. "He had a genetic abnormality, so he wasn't going to live."

"He knew about it. He's saying all the grandchildren have been born since he passed. Is that true?"

Tara nodded.

"He met their souls. Oh, that's interesting. He says he actually talked with them before they decided to incarnate, met them before they were born, kind of like a screening device? I didn't know they could do that. He's saying he knew right away this little one wouldn't be alive in a physical body, and he was there supporting him. I don't mean to say things are meant to be—that's not true—but when a soul comes into a body, things happen."

Tara teared up as her husband shot her a sympathetic look.

"Okay, really, is that what you want me to say?" I asked her dad. "Yes, it is. He says the baby is already growing up on the Other Side. He's already, like, three years old. They can do things like that over there. Your sister will have another baby. This one looks like a girl, and it will be the same soul. At least that's the plan."

Derek nodded. "They all feel she'll have another baby and it will be a girl."

"Oh, really? Well, this one feels like a girl. And he says to not be upset and mourn the baby. When he—the baby that is—realized how much was involved with the body he was coming into, he said, 'Let's just do this, let's be done.' Your dad has been there with him since the beginning, but he's fine, and he knows your sister and you are not fine. All he can say to that is—oh, my goodness."

Tara's dad and the baby were talking so fast, I asked them to slow down. "You know, if you two just want to show me pictures, that's okay," I said to Thomas. I looked at Tara. "The little one is like, blah, blah, blah, and your dad is telling him to calm down."

I was racing to keep up with them. "There are so many animals at my dad's station. This kid is—wow, he's amazing. There's a shaman who says my dog Alki, who died, was a bodhisattva, a holy person. Well, so is this little one. All the animals at the way station are almost fighting over who gets close to him. It's amazing. They're surrounding him. And your dad just let go of him and he's sitting in the grass, and all the animals and my dogs are there. He's cognizant enough now of who he is."

Tara and Derek looked at each other, confused, so I went on to explain.

"This is a really big point. Consciousness survives death, but what is consciousness in a baby? There isn't any, really, not even like toddlers. But your dad said he had a deal that this kid would come straight over, so he's been taking care of him. He said this soul intends to come back as a girl. Let me know what happens. Things change. I'm not sure you should tell your sister. She may end up comparing this new baby with the one who died."

Tara said, "She was already told by another psychic medium that that soul is coming back as a girl."

"Your dad isn't concerned about that, and neither is the boy. Souls keep going on and having different experiences. We've all been different things. I can point to my hips and say there have been a lot of whales in my previous lives."

We all laughed.

"People get upset when they find out they've been animals in previous lives, and I say, so what? It's pretty cool. My dogs and cat and I have been around and around in different bodies. We pick what we think will work in that lifetime."

Tara and Derek smiled at each other and squeezed each other's hand.

"So your sister. Your dad's saying she was always more emotional and that makes her a bit unstable. He's concerned that she's going to look at this new child coming and think for its entire life what it would have been like if the boy had lived. This is the same soul, but he's not sure that's something she should know for sure. That's not his choice; it's his observation."

"That's true, I agree," Tara said. "But she was already told, if she believes it."

I asked Thomas if there were other babies coming. "There's talk of two other babies coming. He wants to know if you want one. One is ready for you if you want one, but you don't physically have to have one."

Tara and Derek winced and shared uneasy glances. It didn't look like they had children on their mind. The things dead parents bring up!

I turned to Derek. "He's looking at you now, pointing out that you're younger than she is, but he says there is one for you. It doesn't matter if you adopt—it will still be your kid. You have a sense of humor and you're really grounded, more than Tara is."

Derek looked at Tara and then shyly at me. "I asked him for permission to marry her."

But Thomas was long dead, so that meant Derek had asked him in spirit. I smiled. "And did you hear him answer?"

"Yes," he said, smiling at Tara. "What happens if we don't adopt?"

"Oh, no pressure, they go somewhere else. There's one waiting for you if you'd like it. Those are all choices. That soul can go to another place. There's a way to honor that feeling of that soul by the work you do, whatever you do in the world. He's not concerned about it."

Tara and Derek looked uncertain. Being told a soul is ready to be your child isn't something that happens every day!

"This is interesting," I said. "You said your sister is in surgery right now, and your dad says he's talking with her. Oh, here she is."

I turned to look off to the right, so I wouldn't be distracted by Tara and Derek.

"I'm talking to your sister," I said. "No, you're not dead. You're okay. You're just asleep having surgery."

I looked at Tara. "This isn't my business, not what you're here for, but what she's saying is—and your dad is nodding—is that she feels she needs to get rid of her old self to get a new self. This is so deep, she can't really feel it when she's awake. She says she needs to be reborn. She's not feeling worthy of being who she is, so she needs to be reborn to cleanse herself. Her guides are saying that her body needs six months before she can be pregnant again."

I shook my head and refocused on Tara and Derek. "But this is your time, so what do you want to talk about?"

They were musing on that when I interrupted. "Your dad is saying he's just a typical parent, proud of you and who you are. You need to take better care of your sister but also follow your own path."

Suddenly I noticed a distressed young man standing behind Derek. He was clearly dead and trying to talk with me. My dad and Thomas both saw him, and Dad pointed to him, urging me to help. I turned to Derek. "Did you have a friend who died in high school?"

Derek's eyes went wide. "My brother did."

"He died in high school?"

"In college. His high school best friend."

"Okay, there's a young man about high school age who died and who's connected to you, and he's here. Who is that?"

"My brother's best friend. Five years ago. We're not sure what happened."

"And his name was Joe?"

Derek nodded, dazed.

"Oh, interesting," I said. "I kept thinking of Tara's dad as Joe, and now Joe's here. Dad, want to help me?" My dad said what I was thinking—that Joe had been murdered.

I told Tara and Derek we needed to deal with this man, and turned back to him. "Joe, if you want to look around, you're not actually in the afterlife. You haven't moved on yet. I know you're here. I can see and feel you."

Tara and Derek stared at me, wide-eyed. They weren't expecting this, but neither was I.

"Here's the thing, Joe. The only thing that matters after you die is that you find your colored door and go through it. You see that gold door? That man there is my dad, his name is Ray, and he can help you. We're not making any judgments about you or how you died. We're just trying to help you get to your afterlife and rest up." I hesitated, then decided to just go for it. "Because ... do you feel as bad as you look?"

Derek and Tara were startled. I turned to Derek. "He looks pretty bad. Was he burned?"

"They never found his body. They found his car, not him."

I sighed. "I think he was murdered. He's almost incoherent." I turned to Joe. "You don't need to be that way anymore. It doesn't really matter how you died; the fact is you're gone. You don't have a body anymore. I'm really sorry your life got cut short like that. Those people around you are your spiritual team. You'll feel a whole lot better once you walk through that door. You'll heal up and be well again. Because honestly, the way you are right now is not the way it's supposed to be when you're dead."

I looked at Derek. "He says, *'I'm so angry that this happened.'* I'm saying, I know you are, okay? We do." I turned back to Joe. "Is there anything you want to say to anyone?"

"Yes," Derek said, turning to address Joe behind him, even though he couldn't see him. "Give us a message for your family."

Joe leaned forward intently.

"He's saying, *'Tell them I did not kill myself. Tell them I did not kill myself.'* He's all bloody and his head is bashed in. I feel really bad for him, because he got stuck. He woke up dead, and he was like, what? He wasn't even quite sure what happened. Until just now he thought he was still in a body somehow. Maybe unconscious or something. He's realizing he has to accept the fact that he's dead."

I waved both hands at Derek and Tara, sweeping them forward to help me. They leaned in, teaming up to urge Joe to move on.

I said, "Joe, we're gonna let your people, your spiritual team, move you on. Keep walking. We're sorry and we're grieving with you, and we'll tell your family that you did not kill yourself. That somehow somebody killed you. It was not your fault. It doesn't matter. They still love you, regardless. They're very sorry this happened. If you move on, you'll start to heal up."

I looked at Tara. "Your dad is standing beside my dad and reaching out for him. He's saying, *'Come on. I'll take care of you. The things I do for my kids.'* He's trying to lighten it up a bit, but it's actually the baby Joe is drawn to. Joe, people loved you, it's okay to go. One more step, one more step. It's hard. Now you're going to get a chance to start over again."

I chuckled, which surprised Derek and Tara. "He says, *'Do I have to come back as a human? Because that was a crappy deal.'* Can't blame him."

They laughed, shaking their heads.

I reassured Joe. "No, you can come back however you want." I glanced at Tara and Derek. "My dad's reaching out, saying, *'Come on, son, you've been there long enough. Come on over.'* Okay, now he's gone, he did it. He's safely over."

I took a deep breath and the three of us looked at each other, stunned and relieved. I described the scene where Joe thought his body might still be. I wasn't sure how accurate it was, because he was so confused.

They both thanked me, and Derek promised to get a message to Joe's family. I then refocused on their session.

Tara had another question for her dad: Did he have any support or advice for her mom on moving or continuing to live with Tara's brother? Sometimes people want answers to concrete questions like this. Although the dead often prefer to talk about bigger issues, like what they've learned, Thomas jumped right in.

"He's saying the divorce was bitter for both of them. He's been through his life review, but he's still hanging out, traveling the universe, having fun. To be honest, he's trying really hard to be a good father on the Other Side, but he was never that comfortable being married."

"Yes," Tara said. "That makes sense."

"Your mother was difficult to be married to—this is straight from the horse's mouth, can't blame me—yet he feels bad, feels he could have lived a better life. He checks in with everyone now, but he could have been more attentive while he was alive, so he's trying to do that now. He knows everybody goes their separate way after death. He feels your mom is stalled on moving her life forward, and she might consider just being on her own, not living with anyone, because he thinks he might have damaged her, soured her about being connected to other people."

"Yes, that's true."

"She's holding off from connecting, holding a buffer zone, so she doesn't have to connect with anybody. If you encouraged her to move out of your brother's house and on her own, she could step out and enjoy herself. She's not living all that she could live."

Tara nodded firmly. "That's absolutely 100 percent correct."

"If he were still in a body, he would advise her to do that. He says thank you. Take care of your mom. He's never going to get through to your brother—he's too analytical. So say hi for him. He shows a softball. Does your brother like softball?"

"Yes."

I smiled. "He says keep telling him to hit it out of the park, whatever that means to him. He's thanking you for having him come talk with you today. He is there in your dreams, so you feel him. He feels more like a family man now than he did, and that was his lesson to learn. He could have been a better dad and human, but he thought he was a pretty good dad anyway."

Tara agreed.

I did a double take. "Oh, we're back to Joe. His guides are thanking you for being here today so we could see him standing there. He's fine now. Without knowing about this, his family will start feeling better. My experience is that once they move out of the Gray Zone, the connections are softer. There is no real healing before that. A big reason why I can get people to move on is that they will feel better and connect better with us when they do."

With that we were finished. Tara received valuable advice from her dad, and learned how much he'd grown and how involved he still was with her family. The unexpected bonus of helping a stuck dead man move on to his afterlife proved to Tara and Derek that the world is more mysterious than we know and that their hearts were big enough to help someone else find peace. They left relieved and smiling.

**The Point:** Sometimes our dead share both practical advice and deep spiritual insight they've gained in the afterlife. They can surprise us by the depth of their caring and understanding, and how involved they still are in our lives, proving that love never ends.

CHAPTER 7

# Walking the Mystery with Our Animal Families

On October 9, 1998, I met my soul mate. Again. At the time all I knew was that I was about to meet the eleven-week-old Cavalier King Charles spaniel puppy I was adopting. When I walked into the breeder's home, the puppy was bouncing up and down, trying to see past the adult dogs. As our eyes met, we both did a double take. Stunned, I heard a voice in my head say, "Oh, it's you," as something in me said it right back.

It took me three years to understand that this dog, who called herself Murphy Brown, was the reincarnation of a human woman who was my childhood friend (yes, *human*) and later my beloved English cocker spaniel Maggie. On December 25, 2001, that same soul again reincarnated as my Cavalier boy, Alki—yes, the same soul in two bodies in the same household at the same time. And on July 28, 2015, that same soul reincarnated *again* as another Cavalier boy—and joined me eleven weeks later as my puppy, Oliver Alki.

I know, you're thinking, *What?* So let's back up.

Before Murphy came, I'd spent many years handicapped and ill, years in which I lost everything—my self-confidence, career, financial security—everything but my family and my quirky sense of humor. Whenever I thought about giving up, I recommitted to creating a life of meaning and purpose, as long as it was fun. In 1998 I decided that fun meant buying a

$175,000 dog (okay, a condo so I could buy a dog, but still). All I wanted was a dog. Just. A. Dog. Some might say the universe had other ideas. The dog certainly did.

People debate reincarnation, multiple simultaneous lives, whether humans can be reborn as animals (or vice versa)—even whether animals *can* reincarnate. Others like me live with the truth: souls can do whatever they want, regardless of human dogma. Souls choose the form they need to do the job they chose before they incarnated, and if everything works out, they succeed. As we all know, though, once bodies, free will, and real life interact, it's a free-for-all, anything-can-happen world.

As I explained in Chapter 6, souls often move together in groups, here and in the afterlife, which means they routinely reincarnate, even if they don't know it. As part of a soul group, my animal family and I have been reincarnating together for centuries, freely bouncing between human, animal, and, yes, alien lives. One time, in ancient Egypt, my ornery Grace the Cat was a woman, and the dogs and I were her cats.

Is this just my weird family, or everyone's? That depends on soul purpose—and luck.

More often than not our animal families are reincarnating with us in different animal bodies throughout our lives. Luckily for us it doesn't seem to hinder (or annoy) them that we are seldom smart (or aware) enough to notice. I'll illustrate with my family, which will give you plenty of ideas about yours.

## My Dogs' Lives

### The Coming of Murphy

Despite my fondness for dogs, I never thought of them as more than pets until I bought a dog who wouldn't settle for that. It just took me a while to figure it out. Murphy quickly developed health problems that would derail my finances, my ego, and ultimately my view of life itself. As we worked through her chronic and debilitating illnesses, I noticed they looked alarmingly like mine. Puzzled and furious, I decided that neither of us would have a life of pain and disability, and went looking for answers. A few other things happened along the way.

Murphy wasted no time dismantling everything I thought I knew about the world. (Really, we should all have that experience!) She was six months old when I noticed that her nuanced responses to people, animals, and the world around her were far beyond what we consider to be animal intelligence. Then on the morning of February 28, 2001, she was curling up for a nap when she leaped up barking and snarling and dragged us out of our condo—about two minutes *before* Seattle was rocked by a major earthquake.

That was a defining moment: I knew my entire world would change unless I ignored what had just happened—and all the other things I'd watched that dog do since we'd become a family. But what was the fun in that? Besides, I was trained as an investigative reporter, am a cynical skeptic by nature, and had just seen there was clearly more going on in Murphy's head, and the world, than I'd ever imagined. I couldn't wait to learn more.

Boy, did I! I studied everything from science to modern spirituality to energy healing and animal communication. Desperate, curious, determined, I was open to possibilities, even ones that seemed dorky to me, the rational, coolly intellectual woman who'd abandoned religion in my thirties because it just didn't make sense. I preferred key lime pie to meditation, liked yoga in principle, and avoided anything that smacked of New Age peculiarities. Sensibilities, religion, politics—I figured anything "given" was both open to challenge and needed it, and the maverick in me was happy to oblige.

We make choices in our lives, and afterlives, choices that define us, that can grow our soul—or not. After much thought and experimentation, I chose to step back on a path I'd left in childhood and rejoin the intuitive world. Although I had never felt comfortable in the world as other people described it, I finally understood why as the human-centric worldview I'd lived in exploded and I rediscovered a living, aware universe.

Of course there was something else involved: the willingness to love. The woman who in 1998 cheerfully greeted the exuberant puppy who became Murphy also harbored a closed, skeptical heart, wounded by childhood betrayal, grief, and loss, and shriveled by illness and despair. I was willing to love, or I never would have bought Murphy: I just no longer knew how.

We figured it out together. Although it took five years for us to heal, years of heartache and humor, we were a perfectly content family: that one of us was human and the other a dog never mattered. I couldn't imagine one thing that would make our lives better, which means I honestly did not see Alki coming.

### Alki: Maggie Plays House

In the fall of 2001 I was shocked to see my deceased dog Maggie popping up around the house in ghostly form—sitting in my office staring at me, bouncing around the room playing with Murphy, even flying through the air. (The things you can do when you don't have a body!) By then I was aware that she and Murphy shared the same soul, so one day I demanded to know what she was doing in spirit form in my office when she was in the living room in a body. She just smirked.

Then April, a Cavalier King Charles spaniel who lived with my friend Jody, whelped on Christmas Day. Three weeks later when Murphy and I visited, I tucked the little tricolor boy under my chin and a charge like electricity ripped through me. Startled, I blurted out, "This one is mine." Jody cracked up and instantly dubbed herself Grandma Jody. Murphy's new brother became Alki, choosing the salty Puget Sound beach we live on as his name. Much later I realized that Alki, too, was the same soul as Maggie and Murphy, and that Maggie's ghostly presence that fall was her good-humored way of announcing her impending reincarnation (after sweet-talking Murphy into trading the carefree single dog life for a two-dog pack).

It was fascinating watching the same soul experience life in two different dogs at the same time: souls are the underlying operating system, and the bodies and personalities are the distinctively unique hardware. Murphy reacted to life in ways we usually think of as human: introspective, observant, street smart. Alki was a goof bucket, interested in food, play, and sticking to me like lint on fleece.

Those dogs had minds of their own, which in no way kept them out of mine, a lesson I learned when I went to the pet store for dog cookies and met a black-and-white foster kitten I instantly knew was another soul I'd known before—Tweety, my childhood bantam chicken. I wished the kitten well and willingly left her behind, but when I got home, the dogs had other ideas, demanding I adopt their cat sister. (Yes, your animals spend a lot of time in your head, so *beware!*) That's how Tweety came home as Grace the Cat.

Most people are necessarily used to living with multiple souls in their family, but it was an adjustment for me. Although she was part of my soul group, and we remember lifetimes together, Grace the Cat was a different soul from the one who runs through my dogs. She was also my first cat, and seized the advantage. Within an hour of walking through the door, that two-pound kitten took over and never looked back. Every time she leaped over the dogs or stole the dog bed in the sun, the dogs would stare at me in shock and awe and I'd remind them that she was *their* idea.

## My Dogs' Deaths

Murphy died on March 8, 2012, of hemangiosarcoma, a blood-borne cancer that is linked to early spay/neuter. We were fortunate to discover it late in December 2011, so we had time most families facing this cancer do not.

Everything I believe about equality and free choice was tested in those weeks as we chose how to meet her death. Murphy refused surgery, and I honored her choice. She was convinced it gave her more time, and that old age was claiming her anyway. She also wanted to fully experience dying—what she called "walking the mystery"—and she wanted me to experience it with her. Those beautiful, sad weeks proved that love can meet and survive death.

We talked about what we would do as the cancer progressed. Over the years as we worked through Murphy's many health crises, we also talked about death, so I knew she had a terrible fear of dying and being alone in the afterlife: "I don't know anyone over there," she'd mourn, which broke my heart. Now, as she slowly died, and as she was supported by all those who loved her, here and in the afterlife, Murphy's fear and worry resolved.

Murphy didn't want me to euthanize her, fearing I'd get stuck in the grief that paralyzed me for years after I euthanized Maggie. But when her spleen ruptured that last afternoon, I cradled her in my arms, saying, "You took it as far as you could, and it's selfish of me to let it go on. It's my turn now. This is enough. We are done." I sobbed my heart out, but I also made sure I was the last thing she saw. After she died, she was instantly in my dad's arms, thanking me for her quick release when only intense suffering was left.

I did not anticipate that turning to euthanasia for Murphy would strengthen me as it deepened the compassion that informs my work. As I watched a remarkable, ancient soul meet death with both trepidation and joy, I learned to look beyond the body to the soul experiencing it and to celebrate the connections that enrich our lives.

Alki's death was a nightmare. Even though his last year was marred by a severe accident that left him with a failing heart, Alki was not ready to die. I don't think he would ever have been ready, but in those last few months I worked desperately to prepare him. Euthanasia was not an option for Alki because death wasn't. That last month I could look in his eyes and see that death was near, and that he knew it, but he refused to go. On November 17, 2014, we were at the animal ER for just a few minutes before he became unconscious; I had just enough time to say goodbye.

## My Dogs' Afterlives

Murphy is as gung-ho irrepressible in the afterlife as she was in life. As she rested up at my dad's way station, she also experienced multiple transformations, experimenting with different forms as she chose her next act. Dad said she made the quickest and biggest changes of anyone who'd ever been at his way station. (Aren't grandparents wonderful, especially when their grandkids are dogs?)

What was her next soul choice? Was she coming back to me in another body? Shortly after her death she offered to, but I insisted she rest up and decide later. She ultimately decided not to reincarnate because she didn't want to risk another painful body. Instead, she would explore her etheric life and wait for me to join her.

These are the consequences of insisting on free choice: we both wept at her decision, feeling our mutual loss all over again. Murphy knew I wouldn't ask her to change her soul purpose for me, and I knew that, once rested, she'd choose what was best for her.

I was adamant about not asking, no matter what. We need to support free choice to promote soul growth, but it isn't easy, especially with souls who were just in animal companion bodies, which can sometimes make them put our needs above theirs. We survive because we are all a bit selfish, but love requires us to be something else entirely. That meant urging Murphy to do what she needed to do for herself, not for me. In case you're wondering, doing the right thing can cut really deep.

With an entire universe to explore and an adventurous bent, Murphy could've chosen something incredibly mind-bending for her next job, and in a way, she did—she chose something that's a reminder of how beautiful love can be. One day she announced that she was going to be my mother for a while. What? She said the work I did separated and alienated me from many people, causing me grief and loneliness, so she decided I needed a mother. Since I had been her mother, especially when she was ill and scared, she was going to be mine for a while, to comfort me. And she was—I could feel her presence around me, holding me until I didn't need her anymore.

Alki hated being dead. He never adjusted to life at Dad's way station. Even though Dad comforted him and Murphy played with him, all Alki wanted was his life back. I could feel it across the dimensions, and one day I saw it.

I was sitting at home when I suddenly looked up and saw him standing forlornly outside Dad's cabin. As our eyes met, he stared at me in stunned disbelief, then raced toward me. As I watched helplessly, Dad ran forward and grabbed him, saying to me, "I'm sorry, honey. I didn't want you to see that. Alki's having a hard time adjusting."

Of course I cried. I was crushed. Later Dad and Murphy

brought him home to me, even as I worried that he could get stuck in the Gray Zone.

They laughed at me. "There are many layers to the afterlife," Dad said. "You'll keep learning. Alki needs to heal with you. This is his choice."

Reassured, I told Alki he was welcome to rest with us and depart in his own time. He evidently recovered quickly after that, because he was back with my dad a few months later, plotting his return. That boy didn't waste a moment deciding his next soul experience.

## Around and Around We Go: Finding Oliver

Souls often show up with very little, if any, help from us. They just know what to do and get lucky (or not). Sometimes, though, you have to go looking for them—and make it up on the fly. That's Oliver's story. Kinda sorta.

A few months after Alki died, I surprised myself by deciding I wanted another Cavalier—and that this would be my last dog. I was about to adopt an adult female from a breeder friend when a grinning Blenheim Cavalier puppy popped into my head, saying, "Hi, my name is Oliver." I instantly knew he was the same soul as Maggie, Murphy, and Alki—and I'd do whatever it took to get him. But he hadn't been born yet, so how was I going to do that?

Not by overanalyzing it: that way lies madness (and quantum physics). This was an intuitive quest, which meant searching for the practical and mystical—a breeder of healthy, well-bred Cavaliers who had the bright, loving energy to nurture my puppy's ancient, sensitive soul. That part was easy. The hard part was getting this man—Andrew, a physician—to understand that I was sending a particular soul to him to be born. (Even I thought I was a little weird.)

By then it was March 2015. Since my dad can see energy lines between souls, I made it his job to connect Oliver's energy to Andrew and told Oliver to "go there." My job was to wait for him to be born—and then figure out which puppy he was.

Uh-oh! Andrew was two thousand miles away, expecting up to five litters, and unlikely to keep all the boys while I tried to find mine. I fretted. Oliver didn't, seeing just a little hitch on his journey home: "We've had a harder time finding each other before," he said. To make things easier we decided he'd mess up his coloring so I couldn't miss him and Andrew wouldn't keep him as a potential show dog (a big worry, since Andrew breeds top show dogs). We settled on a puppy with a blotch on his face and a body covered in wild chestnut-red spots, way too messy for the show ring.

In May the truth hit me: Oliver wasn't just the same soul—he was Alki, coming back with his memories intact. Knowing the horror of his last year, I was appalled.

"Dad!" I yelled. "Why did you let him do that? He'll be traumatized!"

"You're the one who's always talking about free choice."

"In theory, not in practice!"

Dad sighed. "I tried to tell him he needed more time to rest, but as soon as you said this was your last dog, he said, 'That's it, I'm outta here.'"

See how easy it is for souls to decide to reincarnate? Chagrined, I asked Alki to explain himself.

"You don't need to know everything," he grumped.

"Honey, I needed to know that."

"We weren't done with each other," he said. "We need to complete that life together, and I have to finish my work in a dog body. I *loved* being a dog."

The ironies of free choice! "Okay," I said. "I'll be waiting."

And wait I did, for weeks. During that time Alki's Grandma Jody and I easily chatted with him. "Have you been born yet?"

we'd ask, and he'd yell, "I'm coming!" until, in the first week of August, he went silent. Frequency silence, I call it: we couldn't hear him, and no one in the afterlife would talk with us. Grrr.

Since I was winging the whole reincarnation thing, I tried logic. Thinking he might have been born and was too busy adjusting to his new body to talk, I emailed Andrew, who knew I was regularly chatting with my unborn puppy (bless that tolerant, bemused man!): "I haven't heard from Oliver in a week. Did you have another litter?" Back came a picture of a pile of newborn puppies, six boys and a girl. I took that as proof that Oliver had been born. Now, which one was he? My eyes went straight to a puppy as goofily spotted as a Dalmatian, with a slight blotch on his face.

Still, I'm human, and I doubt myself (dang it!). If I made a mistake, I'd miss him. I wanted proof, which meant *someone* had to tell me which puppy he was, but frequency silence continued.

Dad popped in once, saying, "You have to have faith."

"Easy for you to say, you're a dead guy. Which one is he?"

"Believe," he said. "Have faith."

Which meant no one was going to give him up, and I didn't have faith—or time, not with buyers lined up. I wanted to see pictures of the boys, to look into their eyes until I saw that old soul looking back at me. I had told Andrew to watch for a mismarked puppy, so I was terrified when he sent me a picture of a mismarked boy he insisted was mine. Except he wasn't. Now what? I needed help to find my boy, and no one was talking.

Then I remembered that someone *had* stepped in to help me a few weeks earlier—Murphy. I was heading to Vashon Island to visit a friend at her family's beach cabin, something the dogs and I had done for years. I felt sad, because I was now going alone.

Or not, because Murphy popped in and said, "I'll go with you, Mom. We'll play."

"Thank you," I said, delighted. "What about Alki?"

"He's busy getting used to his new body."

"Which one is he?" I eagerly asked.

"You were right all along," she said, laughing, still amused by how hard it can sometimes be for me to trust my intuition, even though I make my living with it.

Bolstered by that memory, and knowing I had to act fast, I threw out my doubts, embraced my intuition and my belief in Murphy, and grabbed my only evidence—the picture of the week-old pile of puppies Andrew had first sent. I couldn't look into their eyes, so I did the next best thing: I circled the puppy I had been drawn to from the moment I first saw it and sent the picture back to Andrew.

Back came the horrifying message: "That's my pick of the litter for a show dog."

See how easy it is for souls to miss each other? Excellent breeders like Andrew work hard to improve the breed; they're not going to part with a potential show (and stud) dog. That's why Oliver "messed up" his coloring with all those spots.

I wouldn't, couldn't, give up, so I offered to accept whatever terms Andrew dictated. I couldn't blame him for hesitating. Sure, a mutual friend vouched for me, but all he really knew was that I was a lunatic trying to buy a puppy I claimed to have sent to him to be born. It sounds bizarre even to me, and I did it.

"I have lots of souls here," he said, baffled.

"Yes, you do," I countered, "but only one of them is mine." I paused. "The world needs more bodhisattvas than it needs show dogs."

Say what again? This advanced old soul that keeps coming back to me is a bodhisattva, as a friend who should know described Alki—an enlightened one, like what Christians call a saint. We worked hard to get that little bodhisattva in a dog body home: losing him to a show career wasn't an option. The upshot? A bodhisattva of sorts himself, Andrew understood the only thing that mattered—that his show dog puppy and I needed to be together. That night in October 2015 when we were signing ownership papers, he shook his head in mock disgust and reminded me that he'd never, ever sent a picture of a newborn litter to a buyer (and clearly never will again).

Now, I don't believe in signs and synchronicities, but apparently when one pops up in my life, I'm ruthless. The picture Oliver put into my head in January to help me identify him? Neither of us knew those distinctive red spots would disappear shortly after birth, so Andrew's "mistake" in sending that picture was… hmm. Despite my doubts and worries, the picture was really all it took.

I found Oliver because I did exactly what my patient dad told me to do: I believed. I had faith that, despite the odds, I could help a soul find its way back to me and I'd find mine back to it. I put my faith in a picture an unborn puppy put in my head, in Murphy, who was the same soul and pushed me to trust myself, and in my intuition and heart connection, and didn't look back. Much.

Not that I didn't want a sign, being human (and me). When I sat on Andrew's floor that night staring at the puppy I knew was mine, I said, "Oliver, I know that's you in there, but could you help me out and give me a sign?"

He stopped playing, jumped into my lap, and flung his front legs around my neck, just like Maggie had done so many years ago, back when I didn't know souls could find each other, or were even looking. Then he kissed me on the lips and pulled back, saying, "All right? I'm going to go play now." And that's how the soul now known as Oliver Alki came home. Again.

The next night we were back home with Grace the Cat and Oliver was sitting on my lap as we called Grandma Jody in California.

She suddenly gasped. "I hear Oliver talking!" she exclaimed, and then her voice got teary. "He said, 'Grandma, it's me. I'm home.'"

Indeed. So, what's next for little Oliver? Like me, Oliver signed up for the unusual (and often exasperating) work as an ambassador between dimensions, from the dead to aliens to whatever is out there in the multiverse (yes, it really exists). His ambassadorial counterparts immediately started showing up, but I sent them away until he could grow up and choose what he really wants to do (besides bark at them, which we all find hilarious).

Is your heart all pitter-pattery? Are you ready for your reincarnated beloveds? Think again: Oliver's tale is a cautionary one. Ollie pushes more buttons than I ever knew I had. I'm amused, humbled, and annoyed on a daily basis (if I'm lucky and it's not hourly). I always thought I was a good person, but now I know I just usually got my own way, which seldom happens with this boy.

Quit laughing, people: this could happen to you. Re-upping with a beloved is a serious commitment on both sides: while you're supporting another soul's growth, you're also signing up for some yourself—whether you like it or not.

That is, after all, why we keep coming back. It's just a pesky detail I forgot in my awed delight in welcoming this ancient soul back into my household. As Ollie. Reincarnated beloveds can be delightful, inspiring, and completely aggravating. Remember that when you're looking for your next animal kid (or now staring in horror at the ones you have). Maybe getting acquainted with a new soul is easier than digging deep with an old one you've known since forever, because you have to be more polite with strangers. Then again, I could be wrong. It's happened.

These days Ollie is wildly kissing everyone he meets, no matter what. Clearly he's a bodhisattva in training. And I, so very clearly, am not.

Here's another thing about our reincarnated animals. Ollie came back remembering Alki's life in great detail. Usually previous life memories fade, and his started to at seven months, about the age Alki was when his memories of being Maggie faded. But a year later he clearly proved that he remembers being Alki and isn't forgetting it, and that could be how it is for him this lifetime. At the time, I was asking Ollie to tell me what he was up to, and he turned to me and said, "I'm Alki."

Of course his soul purpose remains. However, since free will is always at play, what happens next is the mystery that is life, isn't it? That he is having a new life is important. Each body should have a fresh experience: variety propels soul growth, or we're all doomed. As I remind myself (on my better days), he's an ancient soul, whatever the dickens he's up to, and it's his business. His memories and determination got him back here, and now his life awaits. One thing's for sure: as soon as I find *his* buttons, I will definitely push them!

## Kerys, the Russian Blue: Unexpected Delivery

Finding Oliver was involved and exhausting, but at least he was finally home, and I thought all the difficulties were behind us. However, Grace the Cat clearly resented him, and didn't hesitate to hiss and spit while rebuffing all his attempts to play.

"What is your problem?" I finally groused at her.

"You didn't ask my permission to get him," she exclaimed, outraged.

"I'm in charge of this family, and I don't need your permission," I snapped back, then stopped myself, chagrined. I believe that all family members are equal, even if it's inconvenient, so Grace was right: I'd screwed up.

"I'm sorry," I said. "I never thought you wouldn't want Ollie. You know he's Alki in a new body. You liked him."

"He doesn't look like him. He's a pest," she growled.

"He's just a baby. Be patient. Teach him family manners."

Grace was old and unwell, and over the next eleven months her attitude barely improved, although she would occasionally gently pat him on the face when she thought I wasn't looking. Then she had a massive stroke, and after lying paralyzed for five days, she asked to go. Grace the Cat died on September 21, 2016.

It wasn't long before I wanted another cat. Fortunately, I'd learned my lesson and consulted Ollie, who was easy: he'd been begging for a kitten to play with long before Grace died. This time I decided to do what I'd always done with my dogs: buy purebred to home in on specific things. As proof that you can Google anything, I searched "short-hair purebred cats that live long lives, are healthy, and like dogs and old ladies" and came up with Russian Blue.

Just my luck that Russian Blues are rare (despite the misleading ads on adoption sites), and there are two different cat associations, with apparently different criteria for breeding. Since I wanted the "purest" version, I stuck with breeders in the Cat Fancy Association (CFA). However, there was only one local breeder, and they were choosy, insisting that prospective buyers visit their cattery. Which I did—and immediately fell in love not just with their clearly adored and adventurous kittens, but the sleekness of the adults, who looked like small blue panthers. I asked to be on the breeder's list for a girl, but said that for health reasons, I didn't want her spayed before she came home.

That didn't go over well, and they never got back to me, which meant I had to look elsewhere. In January I found an East Coast breeder, who convinced me that a boy kitten would better match Ollie's rambunctious personality, and expected one would show up in his next litter, due in March 2017. (As I later discovered, the breeder was also trying to unload an unclaimed male kitten.)

With a breeder lined up, it was time to talk with Grace the

Cat. What was she up to in the afterlife, and what was her next soul choice? My friend Jody and I teamed up to talk with her and my dad.

"She's stretched out on the porch in the sun, sleeping and watching what everyone's doing," Dad explained, sighing. "She's very bossy."

"Why change just because you die?" I joked. "So Grace, how are you doing?"

She was fine.

"Good. So Grace, I want another cat. What are you thinking? Are you planning on coming back to me?"

No, Grace liked running Dad's way station. His eyebrows shot up as he pretended to be annoyed.

"Okay, Grace, I really miss you, and I miss having a cat. So I'm getting a kitten. It's going to be a boy, and he'll be a Russian Blue."

"Why do you want a boy?" she asked, suddenly disgruntled.

"Why do you care? You're not coming back."

"What's wrong with a girl?"

"Nothing. The breeder suggested a boy would be a better match for Ollie. I haven't had a male cat yet, so I thought, what the heck?"

Grace was not amused.

"If you're not coming back, can you help me with him? Could you look at this litter that's going to be born? The breeder thinks a boy will be in it. I want to know if he wants to come here and if he can be an energy worker like you. I need a cat who can do that."

Grace grudgingly agreed to check him out with Dad and my spiritual team.

In the following days I started chatting with the unborn male kitten, just like I talked with Ollie before he was born. Turns out, we'd never shared a life together, so he'd be a new soul for me, even though he was an old soul who'd been human and a practicing intuitive (aka witch) many times. Curious about my work, he agreed to come and to be mentored by Grace in spirit, despite her crankiness. Brave soul, that one!

But when the litter was born, there were no boys. I also was having trouble hearing him, but thinking he was still on the way, I turned to a Midwestern breeder, who put me on her list for a boy. Her litter was born April 30, and she emailed me that night to promise me one of the three boys. I was trying to be excited, but I was concerned: not only had I been unable to hear the boy for several weeks, but it felt different from losing contact with Ollie after he was born. It felt like our connection just disappeared.

The next day, May 1, I received an email from the Seattle breeders I'd wanted to buy from all along. They offered me a little girl born on February 10, 2017, whose picture was attached. I had no idea I was on their list, and they obviously didn't know I'd decided on a boy.

Stunned, I called them. The litter in question had three girls: one was promised to a pet home, and the day before—the same day the boy was born—they'd decided which of the other two to keep to show. Now they were offering me the remaining girl. Regarding my concern about early spaying, they said they would let me wait, that the important thing was for the kitten to go to the right family, and that was me.

I was flattered, delighted, and still confused: I couldn't find even a trace of the little boy, and now I could have my first choice, a girl. I needed to check it out, so I sat down with the picture of the kitten to see if she was interested in Ollie and me, and willing and able to work with me like Grace had. I was so startled at her response that I called Jody and asked her to join the conversation.

Jody jumped in, then laughed, saying, "You're not going to believe this."

I laughed, too. "I think I will. I bet your answer is the same one I got."

"It's Grace."

"Yes, it is," I said. "She said she wasn't coming back, and yet she did."

I immediately called the breeder back and agreed to take her.

A few weeks later I chatted with Dad, who sighed as he shook his head. "You and your animals," he grumbled cheerfully. "They wear me out."

"No kidding," I said. "I thought Grace wasn't coming back. So that whole thing about the universe looking out for us, it all works out for the best, and all that stuff, it's not true, is it?"

"No," Dad said, chuckling. "It's your ancestors, your *animals*, and your dad. For the record, your animals are all busy troublemakers."

"I'm getting that," I said, laughing. "So what happened?"

"Grace's nose was out of joint when you decided on a boy, and she liked the Seattle people you visited, so she decided to come back there. But you weren't listening, so we had to go all over the country and screw up every deal you made for a cat until you came back to Grace."

I laughed as I thought about it. It was true: I'd worked so hard to bring the little boy home that I wasn't listening to anything else. The whole time I was looking for a breeder, Grace had taken matters into her own paws. Turns out she had gone with me the day I'd met the kittens, their parents, and the local breeders. She had fallen in love with the breeders' kindness and keen attention, and with how healthy and loved the kittens were: as she later said, it was a completely different experience from what she'd endured in the shelter as a kitten, before she came home as Grace in 2003. She promptly decided to be reborn—and was already in utero when I started looking elsewhere.

"Well," I said, a bit exasperated. "She said she wasn't coming back, so I didn't think about it anymore. What happened to the little boy? I'm worried about him."

"He decided to wait and go somewhere else." Dad looked at me solemnly.

I winced. "What else?"

Dad looked worried. "Grace was planning to mentor him, but when she looked into the future, it wasn't going to be enough. Hard times are coming for the planet, and she needs to be there in a body to help."

My heart sank. "Okay, we'll deal with it the best we can. Thanks for the heads-up."

While we prepare for a difficult future, whatever it is, I'm happy to report that I do sometimes learn from my mistakes, and so my family life with Ollie and Kerys is much different than it was for Ollie and Grace. I made sure they both approved of the match (remember that when you add animal family members). As it turned out, the hardest part of that was my ego! Ollie was ecstatic to hear a kitten was coming, and when I went to meet her after I agreed to take her, and then when I went to bring her home, all she cared about was whether I was bringing Ollie to meet her. (Yes, I'm easily amused.) When they finally met at home, they both went for a handful of turkey liver treats and each other at once, and were best friends in under a minute.

At this writing, Kerys, the Russian Blue, is not quite two years old. (Her name means "love" in Welsh, and is traditionally spelled Carys; like all my animals, she chose it.) She remembers being Grace, and is thrilled with her healthy, new body and the great loving start she got with her breeders—and she's already hard at work on her new soul choice. She and Ollie adore each other and haven't had even one spat. As for me, I have the best animal family in the world. Again.

You can see from these two reincarnation stories how complicated it can be and how easy it is for it to go wrong—or very, very right. Souls are busy wherever they are, in bodies or in the afterlife. And even when we humans aren't aware of it, souls are looking for each other—and apparently getting a lot of help doing it. Think of it: how I almost lost Ollie to a show career, and how Kerys was the only kitten the Seattle breeders offered. Some people would call that kismet: I call it terrifying. We came so close to missing each other, both times.

My advice? Decide what you want in your life and go for it. With luck, your animal families will do the same, and you'll find each other. But remember, it doesn't take reincarnation to make a family: it takes love. And that you've got in spades, right?

## Reincarnation and Multiple Simultaneous Lives

Early on I realized that the soul who became Maggie, Murphy, Alki, and now Oliver is not only my soul mate, but a soul that I have spent many lifetimes with, including first appearing in my current lifetime as a human woman. Although this soul has reincarnated as my dogs, I've also recognized it in other bodies, both human and animal, from at least one historically famous human to a quarter horse stallion, a feral cat who tried to adopt me, Alki's mother, aliens, and, gosh, things I can't even imagine (but see, I can imagine aliens). I see it in the eyes, looking back at me, in person and in photographs (ironically, I didn't see Oliver's eyes until I met him in person).

Contrary to religious doctrine, reincarnation happens. It crosses species not as punishment, as some doctrines imply, but because that's the form the soul thinks it needs to do its job for that lifetime.

An extremely advanced old soul like my soul mate's can do an awful lot, including leading multiple simultaneous lives. Is the soul bored, hyperactive, easily amused, or what? It's a mystery, but if we choose a body to grow our souls, those who choose multiple simultaneous lives must really be advancing theirs (and, perhaps, helping their soul mates to advance theirs—good luck with that, my darlings!).

Now, I've met a few humans who were aware of their soul in another human body, either in lucid dreaming or by running into them on the street (can you imagine?), but I've never met a soul as active as this one, and it's mostly in animal bodies. Perhaps it's because animals just don't have as many metaphysical hang-ups as humans, so it's easier to live in multiple animal bodies at once.

Do personalities come back? In my experience, no: even Ollie, who absolutely knows he was (and is) Alki, has personality quirks that are uniquely his, and Kerys is not at all like Grace. The closest you can get is to find that soul in another body, but the exact same personality may not be needed or wanted, and the body's experiences and soul purpose will change it anyway. (In case you're wondering, cloning doesn't work—genes are not souls.) Reincarnation brings the soul back, which is what you loved in the first place. Be content with that.

## Opt-Out Points

Before we reincarnate, we create opt-out points in our life, from none to however many we want. Opt-out points allow us to choose to die when we hit a physical, emotional, or spiritual crisis we don't want to face or don't think we can handle without suffering soul damage, including previous life or serious health issues.

I learned about opt-out points from Murphy. Our energy bodies (our individual energy fields) were so intertwined that we would physically feel or know what was going on with each other (this is never a good idea). For example, I would experience symptoms of a bladder infection and realize it was her problem, not mine.

Eventually I knew when Murphy was considering an opt-out point during major illnesses. Each time I'd explain what was happening and what to expect and remind her we'd chosen to come together, in a safe time and place, to heal crap from our previous lives. Each time she chose to stay and tough it out—until the cancer hit, when she said her next job required her to leave.

Alki didn't bring any baggage in with him, which might be why he didn't include opt-outs. Grace the Cat chose one. Oliver chose three opt-outs, but used one before he was a year old. Kerys chose two, and both are still available.

## My Animal Family's Soul Purposes

Why do our animals come back to us? Soul purpose.

In Murphy's case, I wanted a dog, Maggie wanted to come back as a dog, our souls wanted another life together—and Murphy was out for fun (soul purpose + fun = SCORE!). Also, our shared health woes had complicated our past lives together, and this was a safe lifetime to heal them.

We all also have our own work to do. Humans are so self-involved that we've forgotten that everything else has a soul, a job to do, and free choice. For example, it's fashionable, if myopic, for us to regard our animals as teachers and healers, mystical gurus in animal bodies who are here to serve and save us from ourselves (whatever that means). It's an impossible burden, one animals may take to please us, often to their detriment. That is, the nature of their animal companion bodies can prompt them to put our needs above theirs, which can mean abandoning their soul purpose.

We forget that families do learn and grow together (or should), which is why they're families, and that we all have our own souls to grow, which we alone are responsible for. We also forget that other beings, including animals, aren't limited by human understanding and so readily undertake soul work we may have no clue about, including jobs so huge and strange they're mind-boggling. A well-known animal communicator once talked about animal jobs at an event, then turned to me and smiled, saying, "Robyn's animals have cosmic jobs." Indeed, they do.

The soul that runs through my dogs is a gatekeeper; like me, it straddles dimensions, acting as intermediary between our planet and other beings, planets, and dimensions. It also has its own independent ambassadorial work, and it's a stunner. Murphy's soul choices included being ambassador to the dragon kingdom to help usher in a new era where dragons are physically and mystically back in the world (yes, dragons are real, they're good guys, and they look like ... dragons). At the time this was a job that only a being like an animal could do, because it required a subconscious energetic connection free of human bias. If you doubt it, consider how freaked out you just got when you found out that the mythology of dragons is based on fact: they are real, multidimensional beings (who look like depictions of dragons in many cultures because they were here in visible physical bodies in ancient times).

What's cooler than that? Nothing, really, except how souls come together to help each other, even when they don't know they're doing it. I adopted Murphy in 1998, but did not know about dragons until 2005. In helping Murphy through her opt-out points I thought only of her, unaware of the extraordinary job she had come to do. Murphy was able to do her work because she chose to refuse her many opt-out points and do her job *and* because I protected her and found a way to help an ill young dog live a long, healthy life. ("Dragons?" I asked her, stunned. "There's a job like that? How can I help you?") Because this soul did its job, dragons are back to protect the planet—and they are everywhere.

When I call on her these days, Murphy most often appears as a shining gold human woman. She says she is relearning what it is like to think like a human by exploring human perception outside a body. She also works with me at dimensional portals, supporting me in my work as an ambassador between dimensions, and continues her own ambassadorial work, especially with the dragons.

Alki's soul purpose included being with me, as Maggie so cleverly demonstrated by persuading Murphy to let another dog into the house. But Alki and I inherited Murphy's ambassadorial work together, which continues in Ollie, including his work as an energy healer. What Oliver will actually choose is a story-in-waiting.

Grace the Cat enjoyed being a house cat (quite an advancement for Tweety the chicken, who lived outside and ended up as a weasel's lunch). She, too, explored multiple dimensions in a way that made her what some people call a witch's "familiar." In short, she amplified energy frequencies, which helped both of us make stronger connections to other beings. Kerys stepped into that work when she was a year old, and also now joins me in client sessions as an energy healer.

These are not the only souls who chose animal bodies to do work that we humans can't even imagine, but they are the ones I know about. I hope you're sitting there looking at your animals, wondering what mind-bending things they might be up to, because they just might need a hand up, like mine needed from me. Which you're ready for now, right?

So do families have soul purposes? Obviously. I learned things from all my animals and continue to do so. From Maggie I learned to treat animals as souls. From Murphy I learned to live in a way I never considered, with my soul purpose front and center. From my boy Alki, I learned true love, which is helping me get along with Oliver, his amusing, adorable, and rascally new incarnation. From Grace the Cat I learned to laugh—and to live with an alien life-form, which helped when the real ones showed up. From me my kids learned to fully explore their lives and soul purposes with determination, humor, zest, love—and patience for their less accomplished human.

Could I live, love, and laugh before? Of course. But I learned new things from them, as they did from me, which is what *should* happen. We learned to live in a multi-species family while we whittled away at the other odd, challenging things we set out to do when we found our way back to each other. And so it continues.

How do you help others achieve their soul purpose, especially when most humans forget them when they're born? Sometimes we just have to quit trying to explain it and fling ourselves into our lives—and theirs. By finding a way to live love, we free it to work its magic. And the magic happens.

## Learning Up with Our Animal Families

One of the true pleasures of doing my work is admitting when I make a mistake. Humans just seem to learn better by messing up. Instead of chiding ourselves for a goof, we should hitch up our soul pants and order our egos to "learn up." Our souls are already doing that anyway.

I made a mistake with my dog Maggie. As much as I loved her, I still thought of her as a dog, and didn't stop to find out, on that last day of her life, if dying was her choice or mine. That mistake has reverberated through the years. It taught me to pay better attention to my multi-species family, to do everything I can, that we want and agree upon, that makes sense to all of us—and not just to me.

I've learned to treat my animals as family—as conscious, equal beings with souls, responsibility, free choice, and opinions.

What matters is the soul bond, not the species. Living our lives like this has enriched us beyond anything I ever imagined—and, of course, added strange complications and annoyances. My family is proof that in the twenty-first century the human-animal bond has learned up: it has expanded from the ancient necessity to simply survive to living together to promote heart and soul growth. I hope the same is true for you and your animal families.

Of course, this makes the uncertainty and heartache of loss as terrible as it is when we lose humans, and sometimes worse, if family and friends don't understand and support us. So what do you do when a beloved animal is nearing the end of its life?

## Preparing Our Animals—and Ourselves— for Death

Just like us, animals get sick—and they know it and are often worried. We help by having a trusted veterinarian, researching the problem, and explaining the options.

For example, sometimes a sick animal tells me it wants to die. But does it? Sometimes it does, because it knows death is upon it and it needs help getting out of its body. This was the case with an elderly, critically ill cat who'd gone missing to die on his own and then discovered he couldn't. Once reunited with his person, he was comforted and offered euthanasia, which he gratefully accepted. Another cat insisted it wanted to die, but what it really wanted was to be reassured that he'd get better—sadly, his people ignored me, and he stewed until he recovered.

Sometimes animals don't want to die, but if the end is coming, everyone should know and find a way to accept it, including the dying animal. It's critical that the dying know what's really happening.

Years ago I had an anguished client, Agnes, whose dog, Henry, was riddled with a cancer eating through his intestines. Agnes couldn't let go: Henry was her soul mate service dog, but he was in agony, and death was imminent.

Henry was distraught: he insisted he had to stay for Agnes, and thought he was dying because he'd eaten something sharp that had cut him up inside. He couldn't let go and die, because he thought he'd accidentally killed himself. When I explained that the problem was cancer, not what he'd eaten, he was relieved and accepted death, and his family let him go.

Here's why you need to dig deep: Agnes and Henry had been playing in the park some weeks earlier, and he'd found and devoured a broken jar of peanut butter. The glass had cut him from his mouth clear through his gut, and that's why he thought he was dying. Learning the truth gave him a peaceful death and, I hope, a quicker soul recovery.

Please tell your animals what's happening and why. You will never, ever regret it. Neither will they.

What's right: euthanasia or dying on their own? Only the family can answer that. We need to be clear about what we are doing, which includes learning what our animals want and doing our best to honor their choice—or explain why we can't. I didn't do that with Maggie, because as much as I loved her, I didn't think of animals as souls with choice back then. I know better now.

Treat sick animals like you would want to be treated: with kindness and compassion. Assume they are intelligent, because they are, and they will understand you. Not only will you both feel better, but it could make the difference between getting stuck in the Gray Zone and experiencing a joyful arrival at a way station.

Or it could mean they stick around.

When my beloved Murphy first developed severe arthritis at eleven, she was in so much pain she wanted to die. I personally understand the soul damage that can come from pain and disability, so I explained that she should feel better in a few weeks, but if she didn't, I would help her die. Then I got sneaky.

I said, "When my parents died, we had a big party at their funeral, but they weren't there. If you're going to die, let's have a party while you're still here."

Yes, I was practicing reverse psychology on a dog I knew loved parties. And yes, you know how many friends you have when you plan a funeral for a dog—especially one who isn't dead yet.

As we planned Murphy's "farewell celebration," out-of-town guests telepathically checked in with her. Sure, that boosted her spirits, but the clincher was the food: from cheese to deli meats, I included all the delicious foods I knew she loved, and topped it off with the deal maker.

"Murphy, why don't we have a Costco cake for your party?"

Murphy turned to me, eyes wide in delight, and said, "I think I'll stay for my party." That's how I know that it isn't a deity who saves lives at our house: it's Costco cake.

As the party drew near, Murphy announced that she'd "stay a while" after her party. When the day dawned, she pranced from guest to guest, enjoying praise and food, including that delicious cake. She lived another two and a half years, proof that listening to your animal kids, and responding to them intelligently and compassionately, can be the difference between an early death and one that happens in its proper time.

Murphy's real funeral was a family affair. We flooded the neighborhood with music and, as I danced, and Grace the Cat and Alki bounced with me, Murphy came back to dance with me one last time, yelling, "My funeral is fun!"

May you have the same joyful experience with your animals—and only when it's time.

It's crushing to lose a beloved animal. We get through it by living the human-animal bond as a multi-species family, start to finish. Follow the suggestions I offer in Chapter 11, because whether your beloveds are human or animal, we deal with grief in the same way, from walking them through the dying process to connecting with them in the afterlife.

The difference with animals is the people in your life. Sadly, there are plenty of people who haven't learned up about animals and may not support you in your grief. If you have those people in your life (I don't anymore), share with them if they're willing (soul growth, right?), ignore them, or walk away.

You and your family, human and animal, get to decide what death looks like, from how you meet it to how you carry on afterward. Nobody else. Yes, listen to your support team, but hang on to what makes sense to you and your animals in the moment. It's your sacred job.

Remember, too, you're not just wisely walking your animals through the dying process—you're also keeping them from getting stuck after death. We absolutely must tell our dying animals what is happening and ask what they want. They know when death is near. Like us, they may try to deny it, or they don't want to worry us or leave us any more than we want them to go. But they're animals, and they're also often trying to hide it. It's instinctual—nature's effort to avoid becoming prey.

As I've shown, animals won't die willingly if they think we can't make it without them—or if they think they did something wrong. Some resist because they think they've accidentally killed themselves; some want surgery and chemotherapy because they need more time; some want to die long before their humans are willing to let go; some like Alki refuse to go and their body stops anyway; some like Murphy insist their body is failing and they want to experience the process with us beside them. Ask. You will hear. Let the answers guide and comfort you. You are loving them, they are loving you—and love matters.

## Will Your Animals Reincarnate?

Do we need to know if our animals will reincarnate with us—or already have? Yes, no, and maybe (but you already knew that).

All animals have afterlives, and they come back more often than we think. Granted, some people think we aren't properly dealing with grief when we yearn for an animal to reincarnate. Some don't value them enough to even consider it. Some accept their animals' choices. Others are convinced it always happens, or it's "what's meant to be," or some such nonsense beyond the simple fact that sometimes it happens—and sometimes it doesn't.

Whatever you're thinking, listen up. Their reincarnation shouldn't be up to you: it is the soul's choice made after a life review in the afterlife. It may have something to do with you— after all, look at my wild kids!—but it shouldn't be because you asked for it. It should *never* be because of that.

If you ask an animal to come back, they will sometimes feel pressured to give up what they were really interested in or should be doing next and make service to us their priority. Granted, families are supposed to take care of each other, but not like that. Which is a roundabout way of saying "Grow up, people! Find out what *they* want."

You can learn a bit about it before they die. When I consult with dying animals and their people, I facilitate a "happiness talk" to help both sides reminisce about their lives together as they choose how to meet death. It is both cathartic and liberating.

In one, Felix, a dying cat, said he used to race across the room and do backflips, trying to give his person, Sue, ideas for her work. Sue cracked up: she was a choreographer, and he *had* inspired her. But Felix wasn't done.

Sometimes in these talks animals will ask if they can come back, and their people have always eagerly agreed. The funny thing? They sometimes want to switch species. I suspect these animals have already been suggesting that, and their people are picking up on it. For example, Felix was just asking me if he could come back to Sue as a dog (awkward!) when she said that for the first time in her life she was thinking of getting a dog. Felix giggled, making me laugh as I relayed his wish.

Sometimes animals have to sneak back into our lives however they can. I remember talking with a Jack Russell terrier, Reese, who joined a family because the father and two active boys wanted a dog. The mother wanted a cat, but was outvoted. Meanwhile, her childhood cat, a hairy white beast called Fluffy, had been trying and trying to get back to her, and finally seized her only option—to be the dog. She even came back a lot like Fluffy—mild mannered, cuddly, catlike. With a strong terrier prey drive. Throughout her life she was completely devoted—to the mother.

Our animals often manage to come back and live their entire lives without us recognizing them. (Good thing we don't usually need to know.) The best thing we can do for them is honor them as equal souls with free choice. By celebrating our dying animals' lives with them, and encouraging them to do whatever they need to, we allow energy to flow smoothly so both sides can let go—and maybe surprise each other in another body, someplace, sometime.

How do you find them? Good luck with that! The two souls I live with are very old and crafty. I'm sure some of the ideas I had about getting Oliver safely back home again came from them: they were far too simple to believe, especially when they worked, and on our own, humans make things harder.

If you know they're coming back to you, practice what my spiritual team calls "magnetizing." That meant I was supposed to sit and imagine that I was holding Oliver's puppy body in my arms—make it real by imagining it. I felt better, so I calmed down, and maybe it worked. I prefer big splashy no-doubt-about-it experiences.

Like Mr. Blotchy—the dog that Ollie's breeder, Andrew, wanted me to take, a cute little guy with a huge red blotch on his face. One day, while I was "magnetizing" Oliver, I was sitting in Alki's favorite spot on the beach near our home, the stick-fetching zone, when Mr. Blotchy suddenly popped into my head.

"Why don't you want me?" he whined sadly.

"Honey," I said, feeling awful. "It's not that I don't want you. It's that I want my soul match, and you're not it. You need to find your soul match."

He gazed at me for a moment and then said something I hope you'll remember when you're looking for your next animal, reincarnated or not. "Don't you have the little girl?" he asked, showing me a picture of a blond girl about eight to ten years old.

Stunned, I smiled at Mr. Blotchy and said, "No, there aren't any little girls at my house. You need to work really hard to call her to you."

When I met him that night at Andrew's house, he was still unclaimed. Yes, I tried to help him by describing the girl to Andrew, who stared at me like I was what I'm sure he already thought I was. But am not. Usually.

So, magnetize the animals coming back to you. Imagine holding and loving them. Let your heart call to them, and listen for theirs calling for you, because that's what this is, a heart match. You might have to shell out some money, time, and effort, but that's part of the deal, right? You do what it takes if you can.

If you're lucky, you can skip the complications I had finding Oliver and Kerys and just fall over your animals like I did with Maggie, Murphy, Alki, and Grace the Cat. Like the woman I heard about who lost her beloved cat and then, some weeks later, walked by a store, looked down at a box of "free" kittens, and recognized him back in a new body. It happens all the time. Be ready, be smart, be fast—be love. And, as my dad says, believe. Somehow, many of us do keep finding each other. Our animals are looking for us despite the greatest handicap of all: we are human.

## Rock and Rolling Love and Choice

The soul choices animals make are as complex as our own. However, they often need our help, as family members do.

Would Murphy have achieved her soul purpose of healing past life issues, and stepping into her new work between dimensions, if I had given up and euthanized her at two, as some people urged me to do? No. Did I serve her soul purpose by fighting for her to have a high-quality life? Absolutely. And I would do it again—and I did, by welcoming that soul back as Alki and as Oliver Alki (and welcoming another soul, Tweety the chicken, back as Grace the Cat and then as Kerys).

But I didn't ask these two souls to come back to me, and I wouldn't, because no matter how well we can communicate with them, here or in the afterlife, we'll never completely know everything that goes on in our beloveds' souls, or all the things they need to do. We don't even know ourselves that well. Our job is to love and support them so they can skyrocket themselves into another soul growth experience, even if it doesn't include us. They have the same job. That's what soul groups, and families, do. We love.

In partnership with my animal family I evolved from a bitter woman with a shuttered heart to someone who stumbles and falls and gets right back up and loves again. Sure, you have to do your work, but I was humble (okay, curious and nosy) enough to take lessons from souls that keep reincarnating in my life to explore new ways of loving—themselves, me, and the universe. And to laugh a lot as they took lessons from me. That's what life is all about, right? Learning up.

With my animal kids' experiences in life and death I'm learning what soul choice really means and how many choices there are. There is so much to explore in the afterlife, so many opportunities to grow, so much fun to have, that we should stop and think hard about what we want for and from our beloveds. Consider that when we ask our dead to be with us, watch over us, and especially reincarnate with us, we just might be interfering with, well, paradise. Could you really ask any soul, especially one you loved so much in an animal body, to pass that up?

As we continue to explore how and why we do, or do not, make it to the afterlife party, there's something bigger we must understand: how the underlying constructs of daily life can make or break us. It's time to ask some hard questions about what energy is and how it works, whether we're alive—or dead.

CHAPTER 8

# How Energy, Culture, and Mindset Affect Our Lives— and Deaths

Of course we're trying to live good lives. The problem is the "givens" that can mess us up and get us stuck, alive and dead, especially our underlying beliefs about life itself. It all starts with energy. Bear with me here as I explain: I promise it will help.

## How Energy Works

Even though we do the best we can in our busy lives, we can hit roadblocks and get stuck. Yes, we can also get ourselves unstuck, but to successfully do that, we need to know what "stuck" means by getting a handle on energy, or vibration.

Everything is made of energy: it is literally the stuff of life itself, from human to animal, plant, rock, air, ideas—yes, everything. Energy is easier to explain and understand by defining it as vibration. When people say "everything is energy," they could also say "everything is vibration." And vibration is explained by frequency.

If you change radio or TV channels, you get different stations with lower or higher frequencies because we scale it that way; for example, radio stations 92.5 FM to 108.7 FM, or TV channels 3 to 150. In reality, the frequencies are simply different. Once you're on a particular station, you're tuned in to that frequency and won't hear another (barring murky interference).

When we speak with other humans, we are on a "human" frequency, so we hear each other. "Hearing" means that we are aware of each other and the noise we make when we interact. It doesn't (necessarily) mean we understand each other, because our languages, experiences, beliefs, and attitudes clearly differ, something we recognize when we say things like people are "on different wavelengths."

Ironically, this is literally true, because our thoughts and beliefs are real, too, and so themselves have energy, or vibration. These vibrations have different frequencies, differences we can overcome by negotiation and understanding. The result? Frequencies align (at least well enough to get along).

Now, think about turning on a flashlight. The beam of light flows freely until you put something in front of it that deflects, or blocks, it. Remove the blockage and the light flows freely again. Remember making bunny ears with a flashlight? Cute, yes, but the bunny ears were blocking the light, causing a frequency disruption, or "stuckness."

What does this mean to us? We are the flashlights for our energy, the beam of light, when we are alive *and* when we are dead. We all choose to allow our energy to flow freely or to be blocked, or stuck. We can stand in one frequency and ignore others, or completely or partially block frequencies, meaning we can choose the degree of blockage, or how stuck we are, including not being stuck at all. (Of course, we can also get stuck when others prevent us from choosing, but here we're focusing on free choice.) Any block we run into or create, intentionally or otherwise, can impede our energy, our vibration, and get us stuck. We will remain stuck until we allow our energy to flow freely again.

What gets us stuck? We do. Our experiences, whether they are fun, dull, hard, or traumatic. The things we believe, from religious and cultural traditions to politics and hearsay. Mindset and attitude, especially the biggest thing that underlies all "stuckness"—our belief that we are unworthy of love.

Every single thing that keeps us from claiming our power as loving, worthy beings can get us stuck. Crap, right? It's a minefield! When we die, we take those "stuck" or "unstuck" energies with us, where we are also affected by our reaction to the reality of "being dead."

Still, it's easy to get "unstuck." We claim our power and act on it, from making the best of things, even when we mess up, to relishing our jobs, homes, friendships, families—and ourselves first. Alive or dead, that's claiming self-love (the opposite of ego, in case you're wondering). While we're doing that, we should also change our mindset, but more on that in a moment.

What can we do about the things that affect us energetically, or vibrationally? Besides consciously managing our lives, we can learn to manage our energy boundary, or energy field, something everything has. We know and experience it the way our intuition works best—our particular combination of intuitively seeing, hearing, feeling, and knowing things.

Your personal energy field extends around your body and filters your experiences, responding to your feelings and surroundings. If it's too far away from you, you get interference from the energy boundaries of other people and things. If it's too close, you might not be getting enough information to work with, whether it's choosing dinner or negotiating a business deal. If your energy field is just right (for you), you're doing great, but remember that it's always in flux, reacting to your feelings and environment, so you should always pay attention to it. Once you get the hang of it, it becomes fairly routine. Honest!

You know if your energy field needs work by how you feel and how things are going for you. Feel blocked creatively and can't get a project done? Get uncomfortable in crowds or tired in public? Have trouble saying no to others, or standing up for yourself?

Then your energy is blocked. Fix that by consciously partnering with your energy (specifically, your energy body) to reinforce your boundaries so you are strong, healthy, and claiming your power to live an independent, loving, creative life. Remember, anything that takes away your power is blocking your energy, and anything that supports it helps it flow smoothly.

When you're out and about, living your life, things will annoy and pester you. It's a given, and your energy can get blocked. The question is what you do about it. If you stop and think about what's bugging you, can you change the situation or at least how you react to it? That can eliminate the blockage and let your energy flow freely.

You should also pinpoint the source of the discomfort, because our energy boundaries are always being challenged and weakened by bits and pieces of energy from other people (and animals, buildings, cars, events, the news—you get the idea). So when you're challenged, ask yourself, *Is what I'm feeling or experiencing me or something else?*

Decide what it is and fix it. If you decide that what you're feeling is you, then work on changing your mind, your situation, whatever it is. If what you're feeling is something else, learn to be aware of what is going on around you while not allowing its energy to actually go *into* you and get you stuck. It takes practice to know the difference, but it's worth it. Relax: deep down inside we all know what to do, because working with our energy boundaries is something our souls are always doing, lifetime after lifetime.

The next step is to learn to clear out whatever is stuck. It helps to learn simple energy healing techniques and work with specialists, including intuitives and energy healers. However, you can do a lot on your own with simple self-care, things like taking a coffee break, enjoying a quick walk outside, developing a yoga practice, taking up aerobic sports like bicycling or running, turning off electronics to spend time with family (or yourself), taking salt baths or using dry salt bathing to clear your energy field, working with crystals, and creating rituals to become and stay balanced and grounded. Learn to know yourself well enough to know when you feel "off" or out of sorts or even invaded by outside influences, then experiment to develop ways to clear yourself.

Just remember: we block our energy when we allow whatever it is (and "it" is a lot) to take away our power. When our energy is flowing smoothly, our body, mind, and spirit will feel healthier, more vital, more ... alive. Being fully alive in our bodies (and so growing our souls) is why we're here. Taking charge of ourselves will help keep us from getting (and staying) stuck while we're alive—and keep us moving forward when we wake up dead in the Gray Zone.

It all begins with our choice to love ourselves—or not. However, that's more difficult than we think, because what we think is energy, too, and it can mess us up. Which takes us to culture—and religion.

## Culture, Religion, and the Things They (Don't) Tell You

We live and die within a religious and cultural framework that people long dead dreamed up for us. But is it true and useful? Let's sweep away the preconceptions, from philosophy to spirituality, science, and cultural hoorah, and find out.

Humans have it tough: unlike animals, our ancestors had to create a system to succeed in as they cringed around their fires in the dark, scary nights, riddled with self-doubt and surrounded by apex predators. As they became more successful, they had to justify how the system operated—including who controlled it.

Yes, primitive corporations (aka tribes, civilizations, governments) were born to exert control over people's lives (and, of course, keep them safe, however they defined that). When these groups branched out to control people's hearts and minds as well, culture and religion were born. Somewhere along the way (maybe all along) what was true was less important than what was expedient. Eventually it became hard to tell the difference: we clung to what we were offered because it worked, or made us feel good, or we didn't know better (or all of the above). And we stopped questioning.

Although I've questioned things all my life, I still bought into our culture for a long time. We all do: it's what we know. But what would happen if we thought for ourselves, instead of how people long gone thought for us?

Our culture is our way of life, and it takes a lot to challenge it. I challenge it because I see what it does to the dead—they get stuck because of the beliefs they died with. That means we could be living stuck, too, and often are.

We can do better than we've done throughout history: we can meet the world as it really is. That requires us to pay attention—and to be discerning.

## Truth and Thoughtforms: What You Know *Can* Hurt You

To learn the truth about life—and death—we have to start with a level playing field. Mine is my life philosophy and I'm sticking to it: You're born. Crap happens. Fun happens. You die.

Quite romantic, isn't it? Also no-nonsense and liberating. Your attitude—*your attitude alone, nothing else*—determines how you live your life and what happens after you die, starting with loving yourself. You may want something else to be at play, to hand off authority to "signs and synchronicity," "law of attraction," "the way it's meant to be (or is)," "everything happens for a reason," or somebody's blurred version of the divine, but that doesn't make it true. Right. Or even minimally useful.

Culture is a framework, or structure. We like structure, whether we march to the beat of a particular one or become a maverick who goes it alone (which is also a cultural choice). Culture dictates what is right and wrong; it's the box that contains us so we can do other things (like eat). Bottom line, culture is a group agreement on how to live in a particular time and place (like feudalism in the Middle Ages, capitalism in the last few centuries, and the emerging scarcity/global warming model in ours—yes, you read that right).

When we're fighting for survival, to keep food on the table and a roof over our heads, we don't care too much about who builds the roads or tells us how to think. We don't question an agreement until it's too late, because culture has a dark side, and that's how the living and the dead get stuck.

You influence culture and change mindset by repeating something often enough to create a cultural norm, which becomes acceptable, then ingrained, then establishment—whether it's true or not. Over time these norms, including rituals and ceremonies, become "the way it is." Eventually people stop thinking about it because the norm becomes belief. When enough people accept the belief, it becomes a collective belief, which is like hardened concrete: it imprints on our consciousness and ends in uniformity. This comforts a lot of people, but it is also the first rule for the control freaks. If you want to rule the world, get people to think the same thing—what you want them to think—and to make that an integral part of their lives. Yikes!

It gets scarier the deeper you look. Let's rephrase: when behavior is regulated through repetition, especially through ceremony and ritual, it becomes collective belief, and that becomes true and acceptable, whether it is or not. That's just the way we are. What's more (and even scarier), this collective belief can actually take on a life of its own and become a thoughtform; that is, ideas that are believed and practiced by enough people actually become as real as any other life-form, human or not.

What does this mean? The Empire State Building and Old Faithful Geyser in Yellowstone National Park exist as real, physical things. But the words that define them are also real: they are thoughtforms that have energy, just like any material thing. Take the word *Reiki*, which has been used for decades to describe an energy healing system and now actually exists as a thoughtform that influences us, as real as anything you can physically touch. *Christianity* and *Buddhism* are thoughtforms that have helped many people, so that's good, right? Well, what about the words *Nazism, democracy, monarchy, oligarchy, dictatorship, bardo, heaven, hell, limbo,* and *purgatory*? They are all collective beliefs that became thoughtforms that now affect perception.

Sobering, isn't it? Caution is a good character trait; unfortunately, it's not one we routinely embrace.

Most of the time we mean well. The problem is we forget that what we use to comfort and control ourselves is something we made up and not true or even real (until it becomes a thoughtform). We create a framework—a culture—that works for us, especially in tough times, but it can easily be disempowering. Luckily, every once in a while a maverick slips through the cracks and tells the truth (well, before getting burned at the stake or its modern equivalent, getting laughed at or branded unscientific).

Despite recessions and other calamities, our current time really is not that difficult for those of us in "first world" countries: we have what we need to survive. We do, after all, have grocery stores and house cats. But now we are starting to loudly question established paradigms. This means the foundations we've relied on through our constructs of traditional religion, culture, and government are cracking, if not entirely buckling.

This would be a great time to enlighten ourselves and for mavericks to lead the way, or at least do a little shouting about direction. Unfortunately, we're surrendering to new paradigms that offer rehashed old news: for example, quantum physics is the new science (even though it's decidedly incorrect), and modern shamanism is our cure-all because our ancestors had all the answers (not even they claimed that).

Of course, this isn't the truth: it's the myth surrounding truth. Our ancestors built a world that worked for them, and it became the ultimate answer. Except it isn't, because the old myths are not true.

So you're wondering: *Wait, aren't we supposed to be talking about death?* Yes, but our concept of death is part of a larger construct. I'm highlighting a central problem we must resolve to get to the truth of any issue. That is, to get people to go along with what you want them to think—to march to the beat you set for them—you create religious, cultural, and governmental strictures, taboos, and rules to live by.

Do they work? Of course. Look at the weight of history and culture around us. But they work only until revolutions occur, and revolutions always do. However, revolutions must make way for truth, and not just the latest guru's method for seizing control, whether it is well intentioned, like most religions, or not.

It's time for a revolution about death, because that will lead to better lives (and deaths, and afterlives). How do I know? Because what we have now clearly does not work, or so many people would not be getting stuck. What I'm about to propose does work—it is also the truth, and that's what matters.

What is truth? That's easy. Truth always comes down to one thing: love is the principle that informs life. Love operates beyond rules and regulations to create health, balance, and harmony. Anyone who has embraced love has also welcomed compassion, which rejects and heals the pain that false beliefs impose. Every single day we see the pain that false beliefs impose on the living. As a medium I can tell you there's something far worse: the pain of the stuck dead is staggering.

## Death's Huge Problem: The *R*-Word

Heaven, hell, and all those places religions describe simply do not exist as we're taught, but the idea and expectation of them get people stuck, alive or dead. Something else absolutely does exist. I call it the Other Side, and it includes things I've made up names for, like Way Stations for Dead Things on the Other Side and the Gray Zone. Yes, I've explained the fun (and logical) reasons, but the critical one is this: to successfully create new spiritual and cultural beliefs about the afterlife, we need new, true ways to describe it. This will help us create better lives, which will help us grow our eternal souls—right through death and back again.

Except for your choice to love yourself, the Other Side has nothing to do with what your life was like when your physical organic body died (or your animal body, or toaster body, or house body, or whatever body you were in). The Other Side is not religion-centric: it is just where the dead go to rest up from their lives, decide what they learned from them, choose their next act, and even stay in if they choose to bypass organic reincarnation. Yep, it's a lot, but that's still it.

When I ask the stuck dead why they haven't moved on, they have many answers, but a huge one is religious thoughtforms, which stymie their desire to love themselves by creating doubt and self-worth issues. They are afraid of what religion told them to expect when they died, and because they're in the Gray Zone, which is so different from expectations it's discombobulating, they're paralyzed by fear. They are suffering needlessly, and that makes me angry. I hope it makes you angry, too, if for no other reason than you will die someday and start, or delay, your afterlife there (and so will your beloveds).

I always tell these lost, confused people to look at my dad standing in the Doorway Between Dimensions that leads to his way station, cheerfully waving for them to join him.

"Does that look like hell?" I ask.

No it does not, they say.

I explain that there is no heaven or hell, just recuperation, a review of their lives, and a new adventure. No punishment. Nothing to fear. They look at me and at my dad, they walk through the doorway, and that's it. Just. Like. That. I don't know why they believe me and others who work with the stuck dead like I do, but I'm thrilled they do. The truth isn't that hard. The ideas, the *thoughtforms*, these people lived and died with are.

The thing that makes me angry? They've been stuck in the Gray Zone, unwilling to move on, because the religion they believed in when they were alive either deliberately scared them or chose to perpetuate a myth instead of learning and teaching the truth. It means that, somewhere along the way, religion gave up serving our souls to control us—mind, body, and spirit.

What about the Tibetans, Muslims, Buddhists, anyone with a non-Christian religious or cultural tradition? I wondered about that myself until, in facilitating a mass move of the stuck dead to the Other Side in 2015, I met an Asian way station manager who said that what I saw in the afterlife was correct. He should know: he's been doing his job for centuries (see Chapter 4).

If you're worried that you need religion to get through life, ask yourself: if religion does not serve the dead, how can it possibly serve the living? Then decide what exactly your religious beliefs do for you. Do they help you learn to love yourself so completely that even if you mess up, you still believe in your essential worth? Do they help you become your best self, so you can continue to grow your soul and shine your light in the world? That's what matters, alive and dead.

Remember, we cling to things that block us because they've been around long enough to become a way of life. Most of us don't have the time or the inclination to challenge that, if we even think about it at all. Which brings us back to thoughtforms.

The best role I see for our current belief system, including religion, is as an example of how thoughtforms can block us. That is, being religious is not a requirement for having a successful life—or death. I find that a relief. Do you?

Nevertheless, people accept change at their own rate, and insisting on my way is just as wrong as what I criticize. I say what my heart and experience say is true, to help people understand life and death the best way they can. However, I have also met those who lived, died, and reached their proper afterlives within a religious tradition, including my own parents, so what do we do?

Live and die the best way we can. Do what works. For you.

If you value religious institutions, find a way for love to breathe purpose and meaning back into them. If you want and need to have faith in something, choose yourself, a benevolent force that isn't waiting to smack you into submission (or hell), or unconditional love, which doesn't depend on who or what you are or do.

Better yet, choose a new mindset with equality—and love—as its operating principle. Remember: love is the principle that informs life to create balance, harmony, and compassion, which help heal the pain that false beliefs impose on the living and the dead.

Love literally starts with us. Sadly, many of the living and the dead fail to love themselves. Sure, we all have shortcomings, but we've been conditioned to believe we're not worthy of love, that we're born in "sin" or are somehow less worthy because we have bodies (and angels or "ascended masters" do not).

Our current mindset operates on fear, which fosters dependency. Choosing fear locks us into what hasn't worked throughout history, if the incredible numbers of the stuck dead tell us anything. Choosing love—love of ourselves, of our worthiness, of our amazing bodies and souls—that's what will help us claim fabulous lives and brilliant afterlives.

What matters isn't our culture or our religion—it's our mindset. Could we live and die better if we understood and embraced the world as it really is, instead of how we choose to define it? We can—and we must. Here's what that mindset looks like.

## Planetary Connection: The Great Mindset Hack

The mindset we've lived in, from ancient times right through New Age pabulum, started out with human ego front and center and declined from there. I call it the human paradigm, which insists that humans are caretakers and guardians in charge of the planet, and a "god" or "spirit guide" or some divine "other" is in charge of us. Not only is that flat-out wrong, but it keeps us from being our best selves. That means our mindset, which should create a solid foundation for our lives (and deaths), is our first and biggest stumbling block (which should be obvious by now).

The rest of the planet lives in what I call the earth paradigm, a worldview that acknowledges the equality of all life. In this mindset, which I call Planetary Connection, everything is alive and has a soul, consciousness, a job to do, free choice about doing it, and opinions. I didn't make up this mindset; I learned it from beings who are way smarter than we are (yes, *ouch!*), including animals, weather, land systems, homes, businesses, and gardens.

This mindset changes everything. To understand how, let's look at quantum physics, which says that the world exists because we imagine it. The justification for this peculiar notion is an innocent little atom.

Quantum physics claims that when we observe an atom, the atom moves. How to explain that? With the only mindset science acknowledges: the human mindset, which holds as its foundational premise that humans are in charge, and so human minds control reality. It's an easy leap, then, to assert that when we observed the atom, our consciousness caused it to move. Except...not!

The real explanation comes from Planetary Connection: the atom moved because it is alive. Quantum physics and New Age spirituality don't understand this because they start from the wrong place—the human mindset. That's how we get old stuff dressed up in inventive mathematics, wishful thinking, and unbridled ego.

When our foundational premise is how the world really works—as a collaboration of equals—we get a different answer. The atom is actually responding to our regard with conscious intent: that is, when it noticed that we were at last paying attention to it, it moved to say "hello."

Mind-blowing, isn't it? And true, according to my personal experience working with nonhumans, which is in-the-trenches evidence that cleverly avoids both mathematical hijinks and good old-fashioned hubris.

We don't know this, because we don't acknowledge that the things around us have minds and responsibilities of their own, which diminishes us and all of life. Accepting the equality of all life relieves us of the burden of caretaking and the ego that created it so we can move more easily through our lives. It bolsters us mind, body, and spirit, which is exactly what we need. It acknowledges personal power and responsibility, freeing all life, including humans, to live deeply and completely.

Planetary Connection helps us thrive as equal citizens of the planet. The most freeing thoughtform on the planet, it describes the world as it really exists, so it's true. It respects all life, no matter the form it takes. It gives wings to energy, allowing it to flow smoothly, whether we're alive or dead. And that is key, because living with mindsets like the human paradigm creates limits. Limits create energy blocks. And energy blocks keep us from moving forward, alive or dead.

Does embracing Planetary Connection, the mindset of the equality of all life, mean we won't ever get stuck? No, there's always free will. But it gives us the foundation to eliminate the cultural constructs that limit us while allowing us to think for ourselves (which includes you deciding if what I say is true or phony baloney).

Planetary Connection empowers us to embrace choice and connection, to break up energy blocks and grow our souls. It wraps itself around love, which is everything, because love keeps us from getting stuck, dead or alive. Planetary Connection is, in fact, the very definition of love in action: all we have to do is embrace it. The result? We won't miss out on who and what we could be—or where we end up when we die.

Wow, that's a lot, right? But now that you're clear on how energy works, you're ready for the big reveal: how stuck energy throughout history has blocked not just us, but the planet itself and all beings on it. Let's look at what that means and what we can do about it.

CHAPTER 9

# Energy, the Stuck Dead, and Us: Why It Matters

Now that you know about energy, you can see how it rules our lives—and afterlives. Again, to be our best selves we need to keep energy flowing smoothly by eliminating blockages that can get us stuck, alive or dead. This isn't an intellectual exercise. It's a serious problem for all of us—and for the planet.

Most mediums don't talk about the stuck dead: they either haven't met any or they refuse to believe in them. This saddens but doesn't surprise me: the deeper I get into my work, the more I realize that what I know and experience isn't what any of our cultures teach or what most other intuitives experience. I'm just aware of what's out there.

One of the things that's out there is something I discovered as I started working with the stuck dead. It's an energy block on the planet that has been created by the many millions of stuck dead from every culture throughout history who are still waiting for help. Although we can't see the energy block unless we look at it intuitively, we experience its influence, from our own struggles with self-esteem to disharmony in our families to planet-wide religious and cultural dysfunction.

Imagine this energy block on the planet as a gigantic black vise wrapped around the planet and strangling love, keeping the living and the planet itself from thriving, even preventing peace on Earth. No matter how hard we strive to be our best selves, to master self-love, we can't completely succeed because we are burdened by this energy block. And it's not just humans—it's every single being, from plants, animals, volcanoes, and hurricanes to our conscious, evolving planet.

The only way out of it is through it: we need to find a way to eliminate that block. I have found a way to do that. I created a process to help hundreds of thousands of the stuck dead move on to their afterlives at once. It works because of my crystal, Fallon, the Citrine Lemurian Quartz; my dad and his friends in the afterlife; and the living who've agreed to help and have the intuitive and healing muscle to do it without getting hurt. But there is something everyone can and should do to help: every single one of us can work to get and stay un-stuck and to help our loved ones, alive or dead, get that way, too. Yes, that means you and yours.

Here's how I discovered the energy block, what I did about it, and what you can do.

In one of my earlier conversations with my dad after he died, I asked him how he decided to run a way station. He said that as he was wandering around in the Gray Zone after he died, he noticed many dead. When he told me about it, he was somber.

> **Dad:** There are so many, Robyn, so many, you wouldn't believe it.
> **Me:** So many what?
> **Dad:** Spirits that leave.
> **Me:** Well, everybody dies.
> **Dad:** It's tremendous.

At first I brushed off his concern. Of course there'd be a lot of "spirits that leave," because millions of people have died throughout history. It took a few harrowing experiences for me to understand that he was trying to tell me that gazillions of the dead are stuck and can't move on.

It started innocuously at first. Although my dad said he would help me and my clients by bringing their dead to talk with us, sometimes he couldn't find them, and he'd tell me to "ask them" to come forward. That worked, but I was often surprised when clients said I was the only medium who'd been able to connect with their dead.

Why was that? Because, as I gradually understood, these dead weren't actually in the afterlife where my dad was, so the other mediums didn't know how to ask for them, or where to look. These dead were in an in-between place that I now call the Gray Zone; they either wanted help to get to the afterlife, or were afraid and reluctant to try, thinking they would somehow end up in "hell." To that point it had never occurred to me that there would be roadblocks to eternity beyond the things that religion makes up.

Then the stuck dead started randomly showing up at my house. My friend Jody was having the same issue. Men, women, and children would suddenly show up in her house with their spirit guides, making it clear they were stuck—and asking for help.

Now, the stuck dead will go away and not bother you if you tell them to, but that doesn't solve their problem—or yours, if you have compassionate hearts like Jody and I do. Concerned, we started to ask them what the heck their problem was (in a nice way), and I've covered some of their stories in anecdotes throughout this book. Then I asked my dad to help us, and as we experimented together, I created a way to help ten to twenty of the stuck dead move on at once. But the more we met, the more I understood why my dad said "There are so many." As in, gazillions. I realized that it was literally going to take lifetimes to help them all—and I had only part of one to spare. That just wasn't good enough. Then things took a darker turn.

## The Dead in the Past and in the Multiverse
### The *Hindenburg* Dead

My accidental encounter with the dead from the crash of the *Hindenburg* blimp in New Jersey on May 6, 1937, was a startling personal introduction to the trauma of victims of mass tragedies. In June 2013 I was groggily making breakfast while listening to a TV commercial for a Weather Channel series on weather-related disasters in history that mentioned the *Hindenburg* disaster. As I felt a wave of compassion for everyone involved, on the blimp and on the ground, my home abruptly filled up with dead people, yelling and screaming at each other and at me. It was utter chaos.

I stared, dumbfounded, then jumped into action. Waving for attention, I asked who they were. They thought they were on the *Hindenburg* and that the fire and crash were happening at that moment. They were terrified and angry, insisting the blimp had been sabotaged by a man cowering in the background who they claimed was a German spy. He was weeping and denying it. (Yes, somehow they were getting their information from the TV commercial; weird, I know.)

Shouting over them, I insisted they all be quiet. When they settled down, I explained to them what I had just heard on TV: the crash had been attributed to thunderstorm activity. "That man wasn't a spy. It was an accident," I said.

One of them stepped forward, acting as a spokesman. "What is happening?" he asked.

I stared at him, heartsick, realizing that for them the tragedy was happening right then and there. "I'm sorry," I said. "The *Hindenburg* crashed, and you are all dead."

Shocked, they said they didn't believe me. That's when I called my friend Jody for backup, and she joined in.

"I'm sorry," I said to them again. "It's true. But that was a long time ago, back in the 1930s, right? You know what year this is?"

Of course they did. It was happening right at that moment.

"No," I said. "The year is now 2013. The *Hindenburg* crashed decades ago. You are all dead. Everyone you knew back then is dead, unless they were little kids."

They looked at each other, shocked, scared, and worried about what to do next.

"I'm sorry," I said again. "Let us help you."

Jody and I talked quietly with them as I asked my dad to join us. We explained that if they walked over to join him, they would be in the afterlife and be reunited with loved ones. They promptly joined my dad at his way station.

People I've shared this story with insist that the *Hindenburg* dead were actually in a time loop and that Jody and I simply bumped into residual memories. They said, "How many times have people thought they've talked with the dead of the *Hindenburg*?"

I don't know. What I do know is that this was the last time, since they all moved on to their proper afterlives that day.

The *Hindenburg* episode didn't just shock and horrify me: it was the first time I had met the dead from a mass tragedy, and it sparked my interest in mass crossings. There have been countless mass deaths throughout history, and if they were all as chaotic as this group, there had to be enormous numbers of confused stuck dead. This was the problem my dad wanted me to solve, and I wondered what I could do. It was certainly a logistical problem, the kind I learned to solve in production management classes in my MBA program. It became a real problem I knew I had to solve when I worked with a family with highly intuitive children.

## The Bleeding Grandpa and the Soldiers in the Multiverse

I do a lot of space clearings, which clear stuck energy in a home or business using intuition, clearing tools, and rituals. Think of it as the energetic equivalent of dusting and vacuuming. While all clearings remove stuck energy, mine involve consulting the space itself to mesh its needs and wants with the humans living or working there. Clearings can include paranormal activity, which for me means removing entities, from ghosts to other nonhumans, from the space. That can get, well, complicated.

One of my most difficult cases involved a family with highly psychic seven-year-old twins, a boy and girl. As I listened to the children describe what they were experiencing, I realized they were actually connecting with the dead. The girl was seeing ghostly people in her room at night, and the boy was hearing them talk to him. Of course they were confused and frightened.

I told the children they were safe, that no one was going to hurt them. I said the dead were just looking for help and my dad could help, and if it happened again, they should tell the people who showed up to "go to Ray."

During the time I worked with this family, the twins' grandfather suffered facial injuries in an accident, was hospitalized, and later died from something else. One day the girl twin saw him in the backyard, with the facial injuries still visible even though they'd healed before he died. That meant he was stuck in the Gray Zone. When I talked with him, he apologized, saying he didn't know the children could see him, but he hadn't moved on to the afterlife because he knew about their psychic abilities and thought if he stuck around he could help them deal with them. My dad and I explained that we were keeping a close eye on the kids, and that in his current state he was just scaring them. We assured him he would be better able to watch over the kids if he moved on to his proper afterlife, where he would also heal. Once assured, he promptly joined my dad. Within moments he looked better.

However, the disruptions in the house continued. Despite our best efforts, the boy twin was still talking with invisible entities. He claimed some were human, some nonhuman, and some were in different dimensions, including soldiers who had died in a nuclear war on an alternate Earth.

Yes, the multiverse exists, and I've visited it, but this news froze my blood. We are just relearning how to access other dimensions; we don't know enough to allow a child to explore them. The warrior in me couldn't let that continue, so I took charge and called these dead to me.

"You do not have permission to approach children. You tell all the stuck dead that if they want help, they come to me." I then sent them to my dad.

The stuck dead (who aren't the random or unrepentant dead) are really looking for only one thing: they need help getting to their proper afterlives. Of course they would seek help where they could, even from children in different dimensions. I was now seeing what a gigantic problem this was. Helping a handful at a time move on just wasn't going to cut it. I needed to be able to help hundreds of thousands move on at once, and for the process to take only a few minutes. (Hey, I need to pay my bills, and the stuck dead don't have any money. All joking aside, though, humans stay healthier and live longer when we work with enormous energy in short, intense bursts.)

I thought it was bad enough finding out how huge the problem of the stuck dead was. But then it got worse: I discovered how the stuck dead affect all of us.

As I worked with growing numbers of the stuck dead, I gradually became aware that their condition had created an enormous energy block that was affecting the living and the planet itself. Now, energy blocks interfere with a balanced, healthy, and satisfying life, so this one, made of gazillions of stuck dead, was actually *blocking* peace on earth. That horrified and saddened me.

One day I was discussing my concern with Jody when I said that the only way to clean up the backlog, going all the way back to when life began on the planet, was to help thousands, even millions, of the stuck dead move on at once. As I said it out loud, I felt time stop. It wasn't ego, but simply a "time-out" for me to realize I had a choice to make. Was I brave or silly enough to invent a solution to a problem nobody else knew existed? Apparently the answer was yes, because I did.

Fortunately, I am an analytical, take-charge person who is calm, focused, and can think fast under pressure. Once the idea occurred to me, I worked it out on the fly, enlisting Fallon, the Citrine Lemurian Quartz (whose energy makes the whole thing possible), Jody, my dad, his friends in the afterlife, and a number of other beings.

After the first mass crossing, the goddess I work with chimed in. (Surprise! Gods and goddesses exist, too!) She said, "This is what you and Fallon did eons ago, and no one's been doing it since." Perhaps that's why it felt so familiar: I was bringing forward a skill set from at least one of my past lives.

Of course I made mistakes as I worked out the details, but we were quickly helping five thousand and then forty thousand of the stuck dead go on to their afterlives. We didn't use prayer, we didn't call it "rescue" work, we just took the system I created and made it work, with a lot of help from the team I pulled together. Each bottleneck led to additional breakthroughs.

The snag we hit when moving two hundred thousand stuck dead helped me notice that the Doorways Between Dimensions to the different way stations were colored, which helped us direct traffic, so to speak. Now we can help a million or more move on at once.

Assisting in mass moves can be tricky and debilitating for the living. It's easy to accidentally get overwhelmed energetically and become exhausted, ill, and unable to function effectively; in fact, our spiritual teams restricted the numbers we could help move for a while, to keep us safe. That is why I reserve the process I created for people I carefully train and why I insist it takes only a few minutes (well, I'm impatient, too). And while energy is central to everything we do, proper use of energy is critical to mass moves.

But there's another thing I noticed after several mass moves. Yes, mass moves chip away at the energy block on the planet. But energy is also freed up from this work—it's the residual energy from the stuck dead who've moved on. And these powerful leftover energies are available to use.

But how? Knowing that energy is sentient and sacred, like everything else, I couldn't just fling it somewhere, so I did my usual proactive thing. After one mass move, I looked at the released energy and asked it if it would chat with me.

It said, "I can be used for something."

"Really," I said. "Like what?"

It volunteered to go where it was most needed, and asked me where that was.

Holy cow! Now, I'm too bossy by nature, so I could easily become dictatorial with an offer like that. Besides, we are all in charge of our own destiny, and that includes residual energy. The most respectful, and therefore, best, solution was to look at different situations around the planet and let the energy, and the situations, decide if they wanted to work together.

Now at each mass move, I think ahead to a place or situation that a large burst of energy could assist. After the move I ask both that thing and the energy if they would like to work together. If they agree, it's a match, and I leave them to it. So far the first potential match has always worked out, but if it did not, I would move on to the next thing until both it and the energy are satisfied.

The first time, though, I was not only perplexed at this unusual development but curious about how it worked. It was 2013, and massive forest fires were nearing the ancient sequoias in California.

I called the sequoias, introduced them to the freed energy, and asked them both if they wanted to work together. They did, so I thanked them and wished them well. But I was curious, so the next day I asked the sequoias if they had used the energy, and how.

I was stunned when they said they had used it to bring in cold air to moderate the fires. I checked the news and it was true. It was in those shocked moments that I understood that magic is real and alive in the world.

Imagine what else could be supported by the energy that's released when the stuck dead move on! Imagine what we could all achieve when the energy block on the planet is obliterated!

So what can you do? We can all help energy do its work. While only a few of us work on mass moves, everyone can work on themselves and their beloveds. Learn to love yourself, and learn to keep yourself energetically clear. When you lose beloveds, urge them to let the dense energies slough off in the Gray Zone and then wrap themselves in love and go on to the afterlife. They know what to do, but they often need the self-confidence, the self-love, to do it. Talk them through it, whether you think they hear you or not, because they do. It works. And when you hear of a mass tragedy, send love to the dead and those they left behind. The energy of love will help.

Someday all of that love and support will see the last of the energy block disappear. It won't be in my lifetime, but it will happen. Just ... imagine!

Understanding energy and mindset is crucial to learning to love ourselves—alive or dead—even though it can feel like an intellectual and emotional challenge separate from our daily lives. To make it concrete, let's dive into the details: what we can specifically do, alive and dead, to claim self-love to live our best lives and make it to our afterlife party. Or not.

CHAPTER 10

# Getting Stuck (or Not): How We Mess Up, or Save, Our Afterlives

I've seen the afterlife. I've talked with the dead, from those who got stuck and missed their afterlife party to those who didn't. Let's explore the difference.

## What the Dead Look Like—and Why

Stuck souls hang on to the appearance of their most recent incarnation until sometime *after* they "move on." This means if your body was wounded or impaired at death, you will carry the appearance of those conditions, and the weight of whatever traumas or concerns you died with, until you get to a way station and start to heal. This includes the intense grief of separation from loved ones, a problem that also affects the living, meaning that neither side can fully heal until the dead get to their proper afterlives. That's just the way it is, but it makes my heart hurt (and yours, too, I know). See why I'm so concerned about the stuck dead?

For those of us who see the dead, the appearance of injuries, illness, trauma, and unrelieved grief are sure signs we are meeting the stuck dead. However, healing can rapidly occur once you're really in the afterlife: I've seen it happen instantaneously. Other soul changes are like my mom's: she made it to her proper afterlife, but her appearance didn't completely change until she willingly overcame her self-doubt and did her life review.

What does the healing look like? The dead not only look vital and healthy, but also get to choose the age they want to be in the afterlife, no matter what age they were when they died. That's why my dad now looks like he's in his mid-forties, and why children sometimes grow up. Cool, right?

Even neater, as I've shown, your life before your death always remains in the soul's memory—and that soul part hangs out in the afterlife! That's how we can recall past lives and how the reincarnated like my mom can visit a way station to greet friends and family. Just imagine how many past lives we've had, and how a "soul piece" from each of them stays in the afterlife!

## What Gets You Stuck

When you die, you take with you the energies (or vibrations) of your beliefs and experiences, as I explained in Chapter 8. These energies can impede or help you, which is the difference between being stuck and not stuck. Pretty much anything can get you stuck, starting with the main problem most of us have: we don't love ourselves enough. Here are other reasons:

- **Manner of Death** How we die can throw us off course, including sudden or traumatic death or suicide and mass deaths like accidents, disasters, war, famine, and plague.
- **Confusion** The dead are often confused about what happened and whether they're dead, especially when their expectations bump up against the reality of death.
- **Concern** The dead are often grieving and worried about those they left behind and think they'll lose contact if they move on.
- **Reluctance/Refusal** The dead may have been reluctant to die or may refuse to move on for many reasons, including anger or personality problems (think domineering control freaks). They may be strong enough to keep other souls

stuck, too, by impairing their free will. I've learned that persuading the holdout to move on will free the rest to go, too.

- **Spiritual Team** Sometimes the dead get stuck because their spirit guides lose them. This may not resolve until their teams can find and guide them. The dead may also refuse to acknowledge their guides and accept their help.
- **Life Choices** Yes, we mess up in life. Sometimes the dead were criminals, or were told they were, or made mistakes they believe condemned them. Attitudes and belief systems, especially those that damage self-worth, can also impair the dead.
- **Children** Those who died as children or babies often cannot think too much, because consciousness after death is similar to what we experienced when we were alive. Sometimes savvy deceased family members or ancestors can (and do) call the children over (the living can help, too, by urging them to move on). Regardless, children aren't alone. When I facilitate mass crossings, I frequently see women carrying babies or holding the hands of young children who aren't related to them.
- **Grieving Loved Ones** Sometimes the living won't let their dead go, which only makes it worse for both sides.

## Stories about the Stuck Dead

When we think of the dead, we often think of ghosts, the stuff of horror movies. But unless the stuck dead are the malicious random dead, they're not scary, they're sad and confused.

### The Obedient Child

One of my students encountered a young girl, Molly, who looked like she was wearing nineteenth-century clothing. Molly was accompanied by her spirit guides, but refused to talk with them.

Perhaps they didn't look human enough to reassure her, because she readily talked to my student.

When my student called me for advice, we assumed that because of her clothing, the child had been dead for at least a century, so her mother was, too. We explained to Molly that she was dead and that her mother must be waiting for her, and asked why she wouldn't listen to her spirit guides.

"My mother told me not to talk to strangers," Molly replied.

Heartbreaking, right? But easily resolved. When my dad arrived to help, I asked Molly if she could see him. She shyly nodded. Dad then found Molly's mother and brought her to join us. When Molly saw her, she became very excited. We assured her she was safe, and urged her to walk toward her mom and my dad. As she stepped through the Doorway Between Dimensions to my dad's way station, he gently took her hand and turned to her mother, and they were happily reunited.

### Dead Soldiers

Solders can be intensely loyal and get stuck because they either died in a group or are waiting for each other. Even if they died together, they don't always show up in the same places in the Gray Zone, so they may have no idea what happened to the others and may need to be convinced that it's okay to go on without them. Others are waiting for their bodies to be returned home, which is horrifying: how many millions of dead soldiers might be stuck because of that?

For example, I once met four dead soldiers who looked like Vietnam War–era Americans. Now, time stops for the stuck dead, so they often don't realize how long it's been since they died. To help these men, my friend Jody and I told them that they had died decades ago, the humid climate had destroyed their bodies, and their families knew they had died. That's all it took; they promptly moved on to my dad's way station, where he saluted the men and shook their hands.

## The Suicide

Sometimes a dead person shows up uninvited during a regular intuitive session. For example, Sandy came to deepen her spiritual insight into her work, but a persistent dead man kept interrupting me, saying he was her brother and begging to talk with her.

When I asked Sandy if she had lost a brother, she became tense and upset: her brother Jason had committed suicide, and years later she was still angry with him. However, Jason was so eager to speak, she relented.

"He was overwhelmed by personal issues and can't forgive himself for not being strong enough to work through them," I said. "He's sorry, he didn't mean to hurt you. He just didn't know what to do. He's asking you to forgive him."

After unleashing her anger, Sandy finally agreed to forgive him. Jason then turned his attention to my dad and walked through the doorway, and Dad embraced him and escorted him to his log cabin to rest.

## The Twin

Jennifer and I were focused on her personal life issues when a man claiming to be her deceased twin joined us. Since Jennifer had seen a number of mediums and none had been able to connect with him, she was startled. When I told her what he was saying, including mentioning the intense pain he'd had in the middle of his back from cancer, she realized he really was her brother, Jack, and was eager to talk with him.

Jack had not moved on because he didn't want to leave his twin and his wife and children, and his traumatic death had confused him. After a heartfelt exchange in which Jennifer agreed to relay private messages and they said tearful goodbyes, Jack moved on to my dad's way station. Later Jennifer told me that she had finally become reconciled to her brother's death and could now actually communicate with him on her own, a reminder of how much easier it is for both sides to connect once the dead are safely in the afterlife.

**The Point:** The stuck dead are often lucid and just need to explain themselves—or have their situation explained to them. Even if you're angry with them, loving conversations, forgiveness, and problem solving can help them move on.

## Places Where the Dead Get Stuck

Are ghosts real? Yes, they're often the stuck dead who return to places they knew as they wander the Gray Zone (but watch out, because they can also be the random dead or nonhuman entities intent on mischief). While they are often stuck in the homes they lived in when they died, they can also return to places they enjoyed when they were alive, like dance halls and community centers. The stuck dead go where they're comfortable, and they can be cranky about leaving or just plain confused about what's going on.

I often help the stuck dead during space clearings. Remember, all things are made of energy, so as we go about our day, we exchange bits and pieces of energy with the people and spaces we visit, which means energy gets stuck. Space clearing helps keep energy flowing by removing this stuck energy.

You can use a space clearing ritual as described in Chapter 11. It's smart to do it regularly, just like you clean or pay bills. However, if your home or work space feels inordinately funky or dense, you're hearing strange noises or seeing odd things, or the dog is suddenly wacko, call an expert, because you might be haunted. Here are a few stories to help you figure that out.

### The Dog and the Seattle House Clearing

Emily called me to do a space clearing because her dog Tiko had suddenly gone berserk in her bedroom suite. Tiko was restless and barking, and Emily was convinced her old Victorian house was suddenly haunted. When I arrived I discovered that her home had been invaded by little dark beings that had surfaced from an open portal (think an invisible opening to a different dimension) in the neighboring yard of an abandoned mansion. I cleared that property and my client's home, especially the bedroom and sitting areas.

As I walked the house, I also found the ghost of a small girl who had died there about a hundred years ago. I assured her that her family was waiting for her on the Other Side, and she moved on.

When I finished with the house, I sat down with Emily in her bedroom suite to make sure she was calm and comfortable—"hauntings" can be unsettling! We started talking about her niece Tamara, who had died the previous year at about two years old. As we talked, my dad suddenly showed up with a woman and a young girl. The woman said she was Emily's deceased sister Margie, and that the child who appeared to be around eight or ten years old was Tamara.

Emily insisted that it couldn't be her niece because she was only two when she died. However, Tamara said that she had chosen to grow up in the afterlife with Emily's living daughter, and was changing fast to catch up with her. That is, she had decided that her next soul choice would be to experience human life in the afterlife as a lifelong companion to her living cousin, even though she would not have a physical body. Aren't the choices we have fascinating?

Margie was hilarious. She kept insisting I say things in a particular way, and as I repeated what she said, Emily laughed, saying it sounded just like her. But when Margie rambled on (and on), my dad interrupted her, saying, "Lady, my daughter can get impatient, so can you get to the point?" She did, and what started as a challenging space clearing ended up comforting my client in more ways than she expected.

### Don't Go to the Hospital Alone

I did a space clearing for Leon, who had been experiencing disturbed energies in his home for two years. No matter who came to help, from energy healers to Buddhist monks, it would not clear.

It turned out to be a very busy house. The large fir trees in the neighborhood had been doing their best to help the property clear, but it was stuck with angry energies from the breakup of Leon's marriage and an unhappy teenager who still lived there. Leon had also allowed the house to be used for ritual gatherings that were not evil but did involve the use of hallucinogens and occult techniques that resulted in seriously disturbed space, including wide-open dimensional portals that were challenging to close.

But Leon had a bigger issue. He had been hospitalized for weeks with a massive infection, and four angry ghosts had come home with him. They were people who had died at the hospital, did not want to be dead, and were determined to hang on by attaching to him. I had to forcibly remove them with the assistance of their spiritual team, Leon's, and mine.

Hospital hauntings are common. I hear all kinds of stories from hospital personnel, including ones about employees who refuse to work alone in certain areas, especially in old buildings. For obvious reasons you don't usually hear about this, so consider yourself warned. If you are ever hospitalized, or treated and released from an ER, assume that there are angry dead people who will eagerly attach themselves to you and follow you home, just like those four did with Leon. Make sure you're energetically clear before you go home, even if you have to arrange for your own private exorcism. I am not kidding.

**The Point:** The stuck dead can attach to us or our spaces, so it's a good idea to be vigilant, keep yourself and your spaces energetically clear, and be very firm about being alone in your body. It's yours!

## When the Dead Don't Get Stuck

Being dead isn't always scary and confusing, and no, you don't need to go to college to learn how to navigate the afterlife. Double yay! The dead have always been getting to the way stations all by themselves, because that's how it's set up. The afterlife is pretty foolproof, even for humans, if we'd just stop second-guessing ourselves. In fact, many of the dead never doubt, at least not for long. Why?

Again, self-love is key. Learning to love ourselves while we're alive means we'll love ourselves when we're dead, which gives us the self-confidence to keep moving forward. The self-loving dead are just not that rattled: even though the Gray Zone doesn't look like what they were expecting, many are well prepared and take charge and act. For others, their faith in their religion or culture is so strong that it overrides their confusion or concern about the reality of death. These dead are ready to move on, and nothing's going to get in their way.

Many of the dead are quick and/or logical thinkers. They follow people who look like they know what they're doing, the crowd that appears to be moving in the right direction, or someone they know. Others may hesitate but are talked through it by somebody like me (or a loved one who knows to urge them to go on to their afterlife).

Here are a few stories about the dead who weren't stuck.

## The Traveling Dad

A bereaved daughter, Penny, was determined to connect with her dad, Earl. When my dad brought Earl to chat with us, he showed up with a packed duffel bag and golf clubs. He was reluctant to talk, saying he was moving on, and he urged Penny to do the same. Then he announced he was heading out to golf the universe. (Yes, there are golf courses in the afterlife!)

Penny wasn't having it. She insisted he was still her dad and she wanted to connect with him. When I told him that she needed closure, he gently explained to her that it was time for her to stop mourning and to move on with her life. She agreed, and that happy acceptance allowed them to enjoy a few minutes reminiscing.

When Penny wanted more, I said Earl kept mentioning a blue plaid shirt. That made no sense to her, but she remembered he had blue plaid golf pants. That's when Earl laughed and shook a finger at me, because he had said "blue plaid" and I had repeated it as "blue plaid shirt," remembering my dad's fondness for plaid shirts. Here was a man who kept his daughter and the medium on their toes! Earl went off laughing, and Penny left thrilled that she had finally talked with him.

## The Man Murdered at a Stoplight

Miranda, a client at a psychic fair, wanted to know if her friend Steve was all right: he had been murdered sitting in his car at a stoplight. When my dad brought him to us, Miranda burst into tears, distraught all over again at his horrible death.

Anguished, and in deep, bewildered pain, Steve turned to my dad, asking, "Why?" Months after his death he had still not come to terms with his random murder. Close to tears himself, my dad reached out for him, saying, "Come, son," and held him in his arms as he wept.

Steve's spirit guides explained what had happened at his death. Appalled at the senseless violence, they had reacted by instantly whisking him out of his body and helping him quickly transition from death through the Gray Zone and to the afterlife.

It was so painful to watch this young man weep in my dad's arms that I didn't tell Miranda that part: in a fifteen-minute session you have to choose your moments. What I did do is ask Steve what he had been doing since he passed. I was treated to a startling panorama of an uninhabited alien planet with snow-covered mountains, deep forests, and vast, empty plains where he was hiking all alone, working through his traumatic death. He said he loved to hike and that being alone was healing, although he was aware that his spirit guides were always watching him.

Steve then left after thanking my dad and Miranda, who cried in relief. It turns out that Steve's favorite activity was to go on long hikes in the mountains, so she knew he was finding peace.

### The Dead Poodle

At the end of a brief intuitive session, my client Liz mentioned that she had lost her poodle Mel. They'd been walking in the woods when an off-road vehicle ran them off the path, and Mel had died in her arms. Saddened, I sat Liz back down and asked Dad to get him so we could chat.

Thrilled to see Liz, Mel sat ramrod straight next to Dad and stared earnestly at her. As she told him how much she missed him, he said, "Mom, I love you and miss you."

As she teared up, Mel got so exuberant, he could barely contain himself. Wriggling in excitement he exclaimed, "But there are girls here!"

Liz and I both cracked up. Mel was trying so hard to be serious, but he couldn't contain his delight at discovering girl dogs in the afterlife.

### The Woman's Lost Friend

While I was doing readings out of a local metaphysical bookstore, a woman named Jasmine stopped in, wanting to speak to her friend Stu, who had died the previous week. Stu had no family, so she had taken him into her home to care for him while he was dying. My dad brought Stu to talk with us.

Jasmine was guilt-ridden and grieving because she had been exhausted and impatient and yelled at Stu as he was dying. She felt she'd let him down.

Stu's response is a reminder to consider our assumptions. He thought only family members would yell at each other, so he was grateful to have finally experienced family life. Jasmine was stunned and thankful. It had never occurred to her that someone would welcome our imperfections because it meant they were accepted.

**The Point:** Closure comes in interesting ways. Sometimes we need to talk with the dead to resolve an argument or understand each other. We need to remember that the dead *do* move on, so we can as well.

With this insight into what causes people to get stuck—or not—we get a clear picture of how love allows both sides to heal grief and get closure, to move on by letting go. We'll explore how to do this in detail in Chapter 11. For now, remember this: letting go is one of the hardest things love ever has to do, but when it succeeds, as it did in this final healing story, everything falls into place.

A HEALING STORY

# Family Reunion

Paula wanted to talk with her parents, Hank and Laura, who had died years earlier, and her brother Keith, who had died the month before our session. Paula is a bright, conscientious creative who makes a living as a portrait artist.

My dad brought Hank, who reached back for Laura and said, *"Come on, let's talk together."* But Hank was distracted by all the animals and nonhumans at my dad's way station. He looked at Dad, perplexed, and said, *"Really?"* Dad just smiled and nodded.

"There is a male dog there," I told Paula. "He's adamant he was everybody's dog. Who is it?"

Paula said the dog was Doc. She believed he had something to do with her daughter Sally, because he had stuck with Sally throughout her cancer treatment and then become ill and died.

"Doc is looking up at your dad and saying that Sally has a huge mission in life and this was not expected, so he made a trade-off. A lot of animals take on the illnesses of people. I don't approve of it, but this dog literally took it out of her and into himself. I see her standing on a stage, talking. This is the future. Her experiences are central to this, obviously. She's going to be very practical, talking to families about researching ways to deal with life-threatening illnesses, and very forthright, but it's more.

"Don't tell her this," I said to Paula. "It's like she's an angel in a body. She's there to enlighten the world, to show you can go through a difficult thing and you don't have to lose yourself. Also she is now going through a very dark time and is on the verge of losing her purpose. Because she's tired, drained, she's in danger of burning herself out and spending a long time unable to recuperate. She needs to work on her general health. I'm not a doctor. Maybe someone with minerals, or a naturopath."

Paula talked about her daughter's long illness and recovery.

Then I said, "Your parents are chiming in, saying she's very much focused on the science aspects of what she's doing, but if she stops to remember what she went through without it frightening her, she will realize there is a way of helping people connect to growth opportunities through turmoil. They say they are not prepared to see her anytime soon."

Paula agreed, saying she worried about Sally working too hard, and was determined to make sure she took care of herself.

"So, your parents," I said. "They want to talk with you about self-doubt, that you were always doubting yourself as a child and as a mother. You feel like you're not quite accepted as who you are."

"Yes," she said. "There were four kids, and I never felt I belonged."

"They're showing this, but they also knew you were different from the other kids, and they didn't know how to handle it. They just loved you the best they could, but always felt there was some distance between you they couldn't cross."

Paula agreed, but insisted she had resolved all the issues she'd had with them. Her parents smiled at that.

"They always dearly loved you. They just felt a distance from you," I said.

Things shifted as Paula's mom, Laura, stepped forward.

"Oh, your mom is speaking. It's the first time I've heard her. She's saying to me, *'Your dad, Ray, has a very strange place here.'* And I'm like, okay, yes, there are a lot of nonhumans there that most others don't believe in, and we call them by really horrible names.

"She says, *'Really?'* And I said, 'Yes, really.'

"And your dad is looking at my dad and saying, *'You had the same problem, didn't you?'* and my dad says, *'Yeah.'* What they're talking about is the cultural thing about men not respecting women as equals. Your dad is saying, *'Yes, I was like that, too.'* And your mom is smacking him on the back of the head, going, *'See? See?'*"

Paula chuckled, saying that was true.

"Your mom says she took a backseat, the traditional role, even though it wasn't that way at all. She had him wrapped around her finger. In private she ruled the family. So while he's standing forward and talking, she's standing back with a smug grin. What do you want to say to them?"

Paula said she felt lost when her mom died. She also spent several years taking care of the estate and never found anything personal to help her get through the grief.

"She wasn't expecting to die," I said.

"What happened?" Paula asked. "Was there no choice, on the unconscious or conscious level?"

"No. When your time's up, your time's up."

"The coroner said she must not have suffered, because her face was relaxed," she said. "There was no autopsy. He said she had congestive heart failure."

"Actually, she jumped right in there, showing me she had a heart attack," I said. "She woke up when it hit. She went, Oh my, and boom, that was it, it was done. Your dad was there; he showed up. I'm not a person who says it's meant to be. I want to slap people for saying things like that. You can step out in front of a bus and get killed if you're not paying attention. But your mom is showing me how she woke up with pain in her chest, going into the back of her neck, unable to breathe, reaching out—she couldn't even reach the phone—seeing your dad, and she was gone. Massive, massive heart attack. She hadn't been feeling that great for two weeks, two months. Dang it, they don't watch women like they watch men."

Paula wasn't surprised to hear it was a heart attack.

"She's saying that was not her choice, in terms of dying; she wanted everybody to be there with her," I said. "So she could say goodbye one more time. She says she was helping you and your daughter."

Paula agreed, saying that her mother had helped a lot while Sally was ill and recovering.

"Once she passed, she was in a great deal of shock, but she wasted no time going to the Other Side. Went right through the Gray Zone. She was like, 'What the heck, I'm dead, and they needed me, and what am I going to do now?' And her spiritual team said, 'If you're ready go to the Other Side, you can help and watch and do energy for them,' and boom, she went over."

Paula said it sounded like her mom, but that her dad was an atheist.

"Religions are irrelevant to the afterlife, mostly an impediment," I said. "I meet more dead people who are hung up on that. I just say, go now. But your mom wasted no time!"

"So my dad was there?"

"Yep. Your dad came for her. These two were a very serious love match. A bonded love match. She actually called his name when she had the heart attack and he was right there with her."

Paula smiled, saying, "That's beautiful."

"Isn't that awesome? He's like, yeah, you know. His journey to the Other Side was a little bit different. He was in the Gray Zone, and went, 'Oh, what the crap.' He didn't want to be dead."

Paula said her dad was diagnosed with a terminal illness and died three weeks later.

"Yes, he's telling me it happened very fast. He is also saying he had symptoms of something, but he was ignoring it. To me it's feeling like chest and kidney issues. I'm seeing his chest. It's all black. Lung cancer?"

"Yes," Paula said.

"So he died, and it was, 'Oh I'm dead. Maybe I should think about religion. No, I'm not going to think about religion.' And his spirit guides said, 'Okay, it doesn't matter.' Your parents both made easy transitions to the Other Side."

We both chuckled. Paula was relieved.

"Are there grandchildren besides your daughter?" I asked.

"Eighteen grandchildren."

"Oh, that's awesome! I'm not seeing them, but I'm seeing all these lights your parents are watching over. They're souls. So your parents are still going through their life reviews. There's no time frame on that process, and they're not in a hurry. They're looking at this huge family, at each other, how they related to each other, and how their souls are connected on a deeper level. They knew this when they were alive. They didn't have words to describe it then, they just accepted it. Now they are looking at soul connections, each in their own place, with their guides.

"The life review is like, here's what you set out to do, here's what happened, what got in the way, what didn't. You also see previous lives, and here's where they decide what to do next. What's really cool is they're still looking at options. They see each other at times as they're working out what they're going to do next. Mostly they're very content with this stage."

"Have they been with Keith?" Paula asked.

I hadn't told Paula I already knew Keith was still in the Gray Zone, since my dad hadn't shown up with him. However, I wanted to finish with her parents first. "No, we'll get to him in a minute. He's doing something else entirely. What else do you have for your parents?"

She asked if they were satisfied with how she'd distributed the stuff in the house, like the teacups. "What were they for?"

"Your mom says that in her time you got and kept things. You didn't get rid of things, because you could always use them. You could drink from them. And femininity. It doesn't matter. She keeps pointing out a gold-colored watch in a box. Did you ever come across that?"

"Yes, and I gave it to my sister-in-law. She wears it all the time," Paula said, satisfied.

"They want to thank you for taking care of that, because you are the most levelheaded member of the family. You were the one who was going to do the best and fairest job of that. Did you keep what you wanted for yourself?"

Paula said she had kept very little.

"They're asking if you would do a photo collage for each of your siblings. Pictures of all the kids and their parents. And their kids, if you can squeeze in all the others somehow. But they just want the siblings to have a picture of what the family was like before everybody grew up and left."

Paula agreed to do that and said, "My brother doesn't talk to us much."

"Just give it to him anyway. He has his own road to walk. This is good for you. It will help you make a complete circuit of being a daughter, because you're an orphan. The other thing, they want you to be very careful not to lose yourself. They admire the job you've done raising the kids, six of your own, and what a hard thing it was to help your daughter with cancer. But allow her to walk her own course. They're calling it bunting, like giant cotton balls. Take the bunting off her and let her go free. Pull back and let her go. It's really hard. You feel if you hang on to her, it's not going to come back and hurt her again, and you can't really do that. It's going to hold her back from flying free, and when she flies free, the whole world will light up. This is a very special soul."

Paula sighed. "That's a mom's tendency, to try to protect everybody, but you can't."

"Right." I smiled at Paula. "Now, thank your parents for being here. They're standing by because we need to work with Keith. He's not in the afterlife yet, and we need to talk with him about this."

"He's not in the afterlife?" Paula fidgeted in her chair, anxious.

"No, but let me explain. I don't take clients who call me up and want a session because they're worried their dead might be stuck. That doesn't feel right. But if we're in a session and they're stuck, I'll know it and do something about it. I knew right away when my dad showed up with your parents and not Keith."

Then I asked Keith to join us, and he did as their parents stood beside my dad, watching.

"Keith was by no means ready to die," I said to Paula. "He hasn't completely let go of being alive. There's nothing wrong with that. We'll talk with him, and if it's okay, we'll let it go, but I'm not usually open to leaving them in the Gray Zone if they're ready to go."

Paula nodded, understanding. She said she had managed his health care while he was ill and dying. "Did he think I was too controlling?" she asked, anxious.

"He didn't want to hear that he was sick. He never wanted to look at it or admit it was happening. He always felt defeated by it, didn't think he was going to beat it, and resented everyone else for trying. He had no desire to fight."

Paula started to tell me about his horrible death, how much he had suffered, but Keith became agitated and scared, and looked like he was going to bolt.

I called out to him. "Keith, hang on, wait. Paula, don't go into the physical stuff; it's freaking him out. He was already freaked out living through it. He's showing tremendous fear, pain, and frustration. He actually felt cut off from his life before that. Did he have emotional issues? Did he feel cut off from life before he got sick? Like an automaton walking around. It started about the time your dad died."

"Yes," Paula said grimly. "He was on antidepressants."

I was beginning to get a clear picture of this man and his life. "He idolized your dad. Your dad is weeping here. He could not believe he was dying. Neither of your parents were old enough."

"They were about seventy," Paula said.

"Your brother idolized your dad all his life, but was very shy about it. Your dad got him on a fundamental soul level. Keith was emotionally sensitive but couldn't let people see it. What he said was different from how he felt. He hurt people's feelings without meaning to. He couldn't relate to people."

"Yes, and my sister-in-law said he was so much quieter after they moved out of state," Paula said.

"He shut himself off from life when his dad died. It was like, this was the best person in the world and this happened, so there's no hope for me. So when he got sick, he decided it was punishment and he just let it happen, and that's why he's still in the Gray Zone. He thought he did it to himself. Now he's looking at it and realizing that is not the case: he was depressed about losing his dad. He wasn't as emotionally mature as he could have been. But it's really hard to make a judgment on that, because it's tough losing your parents. So knowing that, what would you say to him?"

"They loved him," Paula said, anguished.

I watched Keith nod. "He knows that."

"Did they take him first because he was so perfect?" she asked hesitantly. She was wistful and uncertain, a grieving daughter and sister struggling to understand her loss and feeling like she didn't measure up. Her parents and my dad noticed it, too.

"No, he wasn't perfect by any means," I said gently. "They

saw his sensitive side so they tried to support him, but they didn't love him more than anyone else. He loved them more because he was their kid and felt it was an eternal bond. He was never going to accept losing his parents."

Paula understood. She said Keith had stayed with her during his medical treatment and it had given her kids a chance to get to know him. She considered that time a gift.

As Keith looked intently at Paula, hanging on her words, I realized this was the moment where they could both get closure. "He's saying, *'How was being with me a gift to you? Because I wasn't there. I was checking out as quick as I could.'*"

Paula swiftly countered that. "He was quick-witted and caring. I praised his faith. One day, we were together in the car, and his wife was walking out of a store, and he said to me, 'There she is, the woman of my dreams.' We shared a lot."

I smiled as I turned to Keith. "Are you listening to this? Are you hearing in her voice how much she's missing you? People do recognize what a wonderful person you were. They understood you were quieter."

Paula described the two funerals they'd had for him, one for the family and one for everyone else. "He doesn't have any idea what a wonderful person he was," she said. "So smart. So funny. It's been a month since he died. His wife said it was the longest month of her life."

I smiled. "He's literally acting like he's hearing this for the first time. Now his spiritual team is talking to him. *'You hear how much they miss you, and how sorry they are about the horrible way you died? It wasn't a punishment.'* He's beginning to get it."

I chimed in with them. "Keith, now you understand that it was this thing that happened to your body. Please don't let it affect your soul. Your soul goes on forever. Where you are now is simply a time-out, where the heavier energies slough off. But you'll heal faster if you simply go through that gold door, where you see my dad and your parents."

I pointed to the right, where I always see my dad when I'm talking with the stuck dead.

"Simply walk through that doorway and you'll start to heal right away. Right now you're not healing—you're still worn out and exhausted and depressed. But once you walk through that doorway, things will change. Yeah, that gold light. My dad is waving at you."

I paused to listen.

"He's saying, *'I know they loved me, but I don't think I was as there for them as I needed to be in those last times.'* And I'm saying, 'Hello, you were the one who was sick and dying.' He's saying, *'I wasn't building bridges, reaching out. I was so horrified about what was happening, I was trying to ignore it, and as a result I was ignoring people, too.'* And I'm telling him they knew that."

Paula spoke up, fighting back tears. "We all understood that. He was so polite, never lost his temper. He felt so hopeless when they said the chemo wasn't working. His daughter was crying. He felt sorry for the doctor. So kind and gentle."

"Right now he's saying that if he stays where he's at, he can try to be present for them. And I'm saying, 'No, Keith, that's not actually how it works. What happens when you are where you're at is they feel you very close to them, but they also feel the anguish and the pain. They feel your worries, and theirs don't ease. Yours don't, either. Once you step across to the Other Side, you'll still be connected to them, but those energies won't be so entangled, and they'll start to heal and you'll start to heal. Which is what is going to have to happen for both sides to move on. You're just in a different place now, but you can watch out for them, connect more easily, and continue your soul's progress by going on.' So, Paula, help me encourage him. Your parents are waving at him, trying to get him to join them."

Paula jumped in and told Keith to join their parents, saying it would comfort everyone to know they were together. "You did what you could," she said. "The deck was stacked against you."

I nodded at her. "I think he needed to hear that. He felt he let everybody down by getting this disease and dying."

I turned to Keith. "You did everything you could to stop it—surgery, chemo—but you didn't do this to yourself. It's what happened. So let it go. Give some last words for the family."

"Good," Paula said, relieved.

"He's asking if you'll tell his kids—not that he loved them, because they already knew that, but that you will be there for them if they need you. You'll watch out for his kids."

Paula assured him she was already taking care of his family and would continue to do so.

"He wants his wife to know that when she would put her hand in his hand." I stopped to clarify. "It looks like during those last few days she would sit there holding his hand. Just holding his hand."

"Yes," she said. "He always knew that when she escaped to the bathroom, it was me, not her, holding his hand."

"He wants you to go to her, tell her to imagine reaching out and holding his hand again, and when she does that, to feel his gratitude for her loving him and being there. He's so distraught at leaving everyone. Ah, so now he's walking to the door, and your parents are saying, *'Okay, come on, it's okay.'* I'm seeing a chocolate Lab? A dark Lab?"

Paula said Keith once had a black Lab.

"Okay, this dog is waiting for him, too. And he saw the dog and said, *'Wait, wait, I know you. I was not expecting that.'* The dog is bouncing around. Keith is turning back and saying to me, *'Are you sure? Are you sure?'* Yes, I'm sure and Paula is sure. If your kids were here, they would be sure, too. Listen to your parents and listen to that crazy dog!"

Paula and I laughed, and the tension eased.

"All right," I said. "He's stepped into the doorway, and my dad has reached out and taken his hand, and now his parents are hugging him, and that is one wild dog, jumping all around, and now he's hugging the dog, too. And the dog is, like, '*I've been waiting a long time!*' They're all together. They're turning back and waving goodbye. He's looking around, stunned. And they're going in the cabin and shutting the door and we're done."

Paula and I sighed heavily, relieved and exhausted. I continued.

"I'd like to thank everyone for being with us today. Your parents are saying one last thing. *'Thank you for taking the time to talk with us today. You do know we've been showing up in your dreams to give you support.'* They want you to lighten up and have some fun. You've had enough burdens in your life. It's time for you to have fun now."

Paula and I smiled at each other.

"You did a good job talking with Keith. You helped him move on," I said.

She did. Paula later said she had wanted a mediumship session because she didn't feel the relief people usually experience when a loved one is no longer suffering, and was concerned about Keith. She said afterward the heaviness lifted and her grief was different, helping her get closure. Her courage in speaking openly and revealing her vulnerability in the session helped both sides heal some of their grief and begin to move on.

**The Point:** Family dynamics and chaotic illnesses can make it hard to say what we feel when we're alive. Talking with our dead can be cathartic, allowing both sides to remember how loved and understood they were—and still are. And how important it is to love themselves.

CHAPTER 11

# Healing Grief and Moving On

Everyone who has lost a beloved, human or animal, knows that love is not for the faint of heart. It's tough to open our hearts, knowing they could be broken if a beloved dies. It's often tougher if our beloved is an animal, because with them it usually isn't *if* they die but *when*. Still, we keep putting our hearts on the line, knowing they could get broken, because no matter what, we want to love and be loved, and love is what life—and death—look like.

Love is the essential experience that grows our souls. It starts by choosing to love ourselves, despite our faults, and continues when we also choose to love others. And that's where the irony of choosing bodies to grow our souls is most apparent, because we know the body will inevitably die. It helps to remember what my wise, beloved dog Murphy said: "We are not our bodies."

Sure, it's comforting that souls are what really matter. Still, bodies are critically important, and often more real to us day-to-day than our mysterious souls. When our beloveds leave their bodies, we are crushed.

If you're grieving, or preparing to grieve, know that you are brave, beautiful, and doing exactly what you came here to do: you are growing your soul by experiencing love. That includes feeling crappy. Yes, you get to feel dreadful: devastation is part of the process and a privilege, because that, too, is love.

Sometimes there's no warning, or you're not there when a beloved dies. My heart goes out to everyone who has lost someone, human or animal, and missed the chance to hold them tight in the moment and say goodbye. Although you can, and should, still say goodbye as soon as you learn of a death—and as many times afterward as you damn well feel like it—many of us get to "walk the mystery" with the dying, as I have with both human and animal beloveds. It is at once horrifying, comforting, and the loneliest experience on the planet. But at last, there's hope, as death is being brought back where it belongs: in community.

After decades of death being hidden away in hospitals and nursing homes, we are now encouraged to be with our beloveds as they die in ways that respectfully honor the process for both sides. As we do that, we realize our ancestors had it right. They knew that dying is a sacred process, that being present with the dying helps them on their journey to the afterlife and helps us live on without them.

They also understood how we die, which we need to re-learn. That starts with understanding what happens as body and soul prepare to separate in death.

## The Stages of Dying

Medical opinion, common sense, and our own intuitive insight can help us understand illness. New services like death midwives and enlightened hospice can help us make death the natural process it is. But to incorporate dying into our everyday lives, we need to clinically and spiritually understand the stages of dying. For that I turn to ancient mystical traditions that connected our lives with the planet through the five elements of earth, water, fire, air, and spirit.

These elements are incorporated in our bodies when we are born—they are the unique combination that is *us*—and when we die, they separate out of us in stages. Death, then, is the separation of the soul from the body, or the dissolution of the body as the soul leaves. Yes, it can be scary to see this happening to a beloved, but it is also both stunningly beautiful and heartbreaking to witness.

Death isn't a lockstep process: we don't always experience real boundaries between stages, especially in sudden death. While the stages of approaching death are also present during illness, they accumulate as the dying process begins, and will accumulate and intensify if the process goes on for hours or days.

Remember that while death is a natural process, and at some point most of us are willing to go, the body itself can and will fight hard to live, because that's what it's programmed to do. Our job is to make the transition as easy as possible, for ourselves and our dying beloveds. Believe me, I know how hard this can be: I watched my dad decline for two years while his body refused to let his soul go. But when death was at last upon him, I saw the stages unfold, and I was blessed with the opportunity to explain it to him in his last conscious moments.

### Stage 1: Earth

The earth element is connected to our skeleton, our physical body. In the early stages of dying, the body weakens. Your loved one may be shaky or unable to fully stand up, or may slide down in bed, even when supported. Pay attention.

### Stage 2: Water

This is the stage when it starts to become difficult for your loved one to communicate. Water is hydration, and now as it dissolves, the body dries out and even acts thirsty. That means chapped lips, papery skin, dull hair, and flat eyes with an opaque or filmy appearance. This stage is unmistakable.

### Stage 3: Fire

We associate fire with blood—our circulatory system, including the heart. As the body starts to die, heat recedes to the core; the hands and feet become cold as the body attempts to survive by keeping its organs warm. The dying begin to lose consciousness, either becoming unconscious or losing receptivity.

This is when "existential angst" can set in: as the emotional body begins to die, worries and fears arise. While we can offer physical, emotional, and intuitive support, death is a singular process, and this is the stage where being prepared is critical. Why? Because this is where the individual's cultural conditioning, or cosmology, can be tested and broken. If this happens, the likelihood of becoming stuck after death dramatically increases.

Doubt is part of life and death, and doubt can rule this stage of dying: the body doesn't want to die even if it's failing, and it struggles. Doubt tests faith as well, so whatever our beliefs in spirit guides, guardian angels, deities, or religious traditions may be when we're fully functioning, this stage challenges belief and certainty.

We support our dying in this stage by asking our own spiritual team and theirs to step in and help (yes, we can all do this). Their team is trying to help, but the confusion that accompanies the dying process can mean the dying refuse their support because they no longer recognize them (if they ever did). An all-hands-on-deck spiritual perspective can help the dying successfully transition, and just in time, too—once the fire stage sets in, active dying begins.

### Stage 4: Air

As the element air recedes, the dying person cannot breathe normally. The time between breaths increases, breathing is intermittent, or it is shallow and fast paced for a few beats before it slows. Very little air is going in at this point, and it leaves in gasps or gentle waves. It ends in a final exhalation: death.

## Stage 5: Spirit

The body is dead, but the soul may temporarily remain, perhaps for hours or even days, as some spiritual traditions maintain. Nevertheless, in the spirit stage there is a complete dissolution of the body and soul. The body cannot be revived, and it is time for the soul to leave.

While the living are left to grieve, they should also be vigilant, because the soul may need guidance. Many of the dead tell me death confused them: since they were still able to see and hear the living, they often didn't realize they had died. Even if they know, this may still be a perplexing time. They may be relieved to be free of the dying process but still grieving that it actually happened.

A lot can happen at this stage to throw the dead off the afterlife trail so they miss that party my dad is so fond of, so here's some straightforward advice. Yes, you the living are grieving your loss, but think first of your dead. Tell them point-blank they are dead: explain what happened, tell them to accept their spiritual team, which is surrounding them to help, and urge them to move on.

This is so important, I must emphasize it. Whether you're with your beloveds when they die, or hear about it later, or even if it is years later and it's just now occurring to you, talk to them as if they are right there beside you. Say something like, "You're dead. Goodbye. I love you. Love yourself. Slough off those denser earth energies. Find your doorway, and go already." Believe me. It matters: to them, and to you.

You can do this while performing whatever death ritual works for you, especially if it's one you worked out with the dying ahead of time. The ritual will help both sides get clarity and connection. It could include mantras, prayers, incense, candles, holding hands, whatever you devise together that honors both sides.

## Death and the Daily Prompts

While death frequently takes us by surprise, we should still prep for it (avoiding it won't work). What can we do to live healthy, balanced, well-ordered lives that recognize they will end?

As trite as it may sound, it helps to practice gratitude every day for every little thing that goes well (or at least all right, or is just plain over). Acknowledging the simple, benign details gets us through the days—and to the far side of grief after a death occurs.

Gratitude includes appreciating those who are in our lives, even if they occasionally (or usually) aggravate us, because, hello, human! Always let your beloveds know you appreciate and will miss them when you die, even if you're just fine, because you never know.

I learned this as a kid from my dad's parents. After every annual visit, they made a point of saying, "We're getting older and may die before we see you again, so know that we love you." I used to giggle at this quirky ritual, not knowing what else to make of it. Then my brother died unexpectedly, followed by several beloved adults, and I realized that my grandparents were crazy smart to say their goodbyes in person. As it turned out, they both died when I wasn't around, and all I got was a funeral—and the memories of those savvy childhood farewells. So please, say goodbye before you can't, and encourage your beloveds to do the same thing.

In fact, why don't we create a holiday to celebrate life and death with our living and dead beloveds? Yep, let's start the afterlife party early! I honestly think that would help our culture have a better relationship with death, even make it normal again. Have a nice meal, set a place for everyone, including the dead, and create a ritual to say hello and goodbye. It would take the time—an entire day in our over-packed lives—to acknowledge death as part of life, honor our dead, and celebrate our mortality while contemplating what we still want to accomplish. Imagine the Day of the Dead, Valentine's Day, Thanksgiving, and life coaching all rolled into one holiday. With chocolate and cherry pie.

I'm serious. Many of the stuck dead I meet didn't get a chance to say goodbye, so both sides have a harder time moving on. If we made recognizing the fragility of life part of our operating philosophy, then when death occurs, especially if it takes us by surprise, we would at least remember that we previewed goodbye. I swear it works.

## Preparing for Death and Grief

It's hard to say goodbye to a beloved, human or animal. It can be harder to live the goodbye, but it's possible, from walking them through the dying process to connecting with them in the afterlife. Be practical, careful, sensible, loving, wildly intuitive, and even spiritual, if that means something to you, and follow these tips.

### You're a Family

Remember that you're a family, even if you're the only one left. Yes, the dying person or animal comes first, as any proper hospice model should tell you, but prepare everyone (including yourself) by seeing to individual needs as best you can. Barring a sudden, unexpected death, they all know it's coming and react according to their unique personalities. Guilt, worry, concern, fear, and jealousy can all show up—and amazing compassion as well.

### Build Community

You can and should ask for help from friends and family. Be clear that anyone you ask can refuse. It's interesting, painful, and exhilarating to see who shows up, who doesn't, and what new connections you make. People often mean well, but our culture is big on avoiding feelings, and dying well requires feelings. Your community will feel with you. The rest, well, you'll be surprised by those who don't, especially when it's dying animals. That's their mindset, not yours. Forgive and move on. Or out.

### Do Your Homework

Help yourself and your beloveds understand and accept the dying process. Figure out what it takes to care for your dying and what makes sense, decide what to do, and see that it gets done. Listen up: do whatever you have to do so you and yours can live with it afterward.

You and your family, human and animal, get to decide what death looks like, from how you meet it to how you carry on afterward. Nobody else. Yes, listen to others—your medical team, spiritual counselors, psychotherapists, intuitives, energy healers, hospice and grief-support professionals, family, and friends—and hang on to what makes sense to you and to your dying beloveds in the moment. That's all any of us can do—and all the dying really ask of us.

Having experienced my brother's death with absolutely no warning, I'm a strong advocate for preparing children for their own and a sibling's death—for any death, human or animal. It's gut wrenching but necessary. For example, did you know that a common feeling among surviving children is that they were responsible for a sibling's death, even if it was an illness? Learn from my unnecessary and debilitating angst: I knew better, even at nine, but that peculiar, unearned guilt haunted me for at least fifteen years. You have to choose how you face dying and death (and the afterlife), and if you're a parent, you're choosing for everyone. So wise up.

With luck you'll get to accompany an animal through old age. What can you manage, afford, and stand? How do you explain it to your animal, the rest of the family, and yourself? Before you even get an animal, consider how and why your family will walk that last road together, because it always ends one way—in heartbreak. If that makes you flinch, excellent: it means you're thinking. You'll figure out a way to get through it, because that's what life is all about. Life with an aging animal is magnificent. You will experience mystery, frustration, exhaustion, and grief, but if you're looking for grace in action, this is it.

### Don't Buy into the Guilt

The current medical establishment believes that fighting death, no matter the odds or the suffering involved, is more important than a life well lived and a death gently met. Someday the system will grow up. In the meantime, you be a grown-up for it. Pain, suffering, and disability are cruel things. You will know when enough is enough. You cannot beat death. You *can* make it acceptable—even glorious.

If you live somewhere where humans can choose to end their lives, discuss this option with beloveds and support their choice. For your animals, yes, you'll feel bad if you resort to euthanasia and you haven't sorted through the whys and why-nots with them, yourself, and the rest of the family. You'll feel bad if you don't and drag out an ending that causes misery for no good reason. You'll feel bad, regardless.

Figure out what the limits are for both the dying and the living. Walk away from anyone who tries to make you feel guilty for choosing to meet death on your own terms and supporting your dying beloveds the same way. Hospice is learning, even with animals, but be careful of animal hospice, because some of those people still don't understand mercy.

Figure out what love looks like to you and to the rest of the family, from the first day to the last. Cling to it.

### Stay Present

We can get caught up in thinking about the past and the future—about what life was like before dying showed up, and what it will be like afterward. That's normal. But be careful: don't miss the "now" of the dying process. Walk the mystery with your beloveds. You'll be exhilarated and crushed, but you'll also never regret it.

### Get a Great Team

Dying can and should be a community event, starting with your own support team. That includes doctors and veterinarians, social workers, counselors, ministers, and sitters—yes, people who can be with your dying so you can get a break (and a nap). Always remember that the team is your partner, but you and your dying are in charge. If you're in charge, either as the animal owner or as the person with medical power of attorney, you make the decisions for and with your dying, if they are lucid. Fire anyone who thinks otherwise.

I believe your team should include an energy healer and a professional intuitive, and not just because I am one. An energy healer can help you follow the vibration I discussed in Chapter 8. While there are many energy healing modalities to choose from, you can also put hands on your beloveds and yourself and invite healing energy to support the dying and those left behind.

If you are a healer and/or an intuitive, hire someone else: you need a compassionate, objective outsider. I hired an intuitive for the deaths of each of my animals. She gave me additional perspective on the tough issues and enriched my family's last days together. I know that neither I nor my beloveds would have done as well without that loving woman who confirmed my own insights, added others, helped us say goodbye, and was simply there as I howled with grief and loss. You hear the medical from the medical team, what you want (or not) from family and friends, what you fear from yourself, and what love has to say from your heart—and an intuitive and healer.

### Schedule Self-Care

Caught up in our beloved's dying process, we often forget to take care of ourselves first, a mistake that can lead to illness and despair. We can't help ourselves, our dying, or others, especially children, if we're worn out. Take time for yourself, whatever that means in the moment: take a walk, a nap, or time to think; light a candle; dance; read a book; sleep; eat. It's important. Put aside your ego, that part of you that thinks you can tough it out and go it alone or ignore your needs. It's not just okay to be vulnerable, to need support, to bolster mind, body, and spirit—it's part of the job of being human. Especially when a beloved is dying.

### Schedule Venting

You stay sane by letting out the fear, anger, grief, and everything else you're feeling as you helplessly watch a beloved die, so schedule time to do just that. Try starting with twenty-minute blowouts: set a timer and scream, yell, cry, throw things, whatever it takes to vent. When the buzzer goes off, dry your eyes, buck up, and get back to your living and dying beloveds. Yes, it works, before and after a death. I'm proof.

## After Death

Your beloved is gone. You're exhausted, grieving, in shock, lost, confused, relieved it's over, and probably desperate for sleep. But you still have work to do—and so does your beloved. These tips will help both sides heal grief and move on.

### Throw a Spectacular Funeral—Even if It's Just You

Funerals help both sides, the living and dead, let go, get closure, and move on. Funerals are community events that give friends, family, business associates, and the morbidly curious an opportunity to collectively remember, honor, and celebrate the deceased while supporting both the bereaved and the community. While giving us the time to consider the role of death in our lives, funerals help keep energy moving freely, which is critical.

Funerals are also important for the dead, who come back for them. After all, it's their farewell party! Funerals give the dead the chance to say goodbye, even if no one is listening. In fact, their spiritual team often encourages them to attend their funeral to get closure and see how the living are doing. I've talked to some hilarious, feisty dead who actually went to their funerals to tally up who bothered to come—and who did not. So honor your dead and those left behind by throwing the most spectacular, teary, blowout funeral you can. Your dead will love it. So will you.

I find it unbelievably selfish for the dying to insist there be no funeral—and curiously weird for the living to go along with it. The dead will discover that there's something missing, and the survivors are left hanging, with no outlet for their grief (or annoyance).

Ignore those (arrogant and controlling) wishes and throw a funeral that honors the spirit and personality of the deceased—because, let's be real: sometimes we're just glad it's over, a funeral acknowledges that, and it's more than okay, it's right. If you have to, throw a funeral for a beloved in the privacy of your home, whenever you feel like it, even if years have gone by since they died. Let your common sense and intuition guide you, even work out some details with your dying beloveds if you can. You'll be grateful when the time comes. Trust me, so will they—even the ornery ones, still trying to control us from beyond the grave.

## Honor and Celebrate Your Dead

Remember your dead whenever you want, even daily, and certainly on the anniversary of their deaths, birthdays, adoption days, and any other landmark days. At some point the pain will lessen, and you may even discover that a day or two goes by when you don't think about them, or that doing so makes you smile. Treasure it all. It's life. But don't hang on to them. If you don't let them go, they'll have a harder time moving on, and so will you. The vibration of attachment can be a lead weight that sinks their happiness and forward movement—and yours. Honor and celebrate, yes, but kick their butts into the afterlife while kicking yours along the road called What's Next.

## Ask Them to Chime In

Sure, go ahead and ask them for a sign, but be careful: believing that signs are necessary, and waiting for them, can trap us in grief when we should be moving through it. I'm not big on signs and synchronicities, but they sometimes show up anyway.

I remember being chagrined by the message but telling some clients that their sister said she would send them a white feather as proof she was okay, because, dang it, it's always a white feather, and it's beyond corny. I didn't blame them for rolling their eyes (I restrained myself—I think). The laugh was on all of us: as they walked away, a white feather drifted down and landed on the sidewalk. Take that to mean if you get a sign, consider it a lucky break and be grateful that you cared enough to ask for one in the first place—and that your beloveds have a sense of humor.

Instead of asking for a sign, why not just go ahead and ask them to connect with you? Connecting doesn't mean holding them back from the afterlife; it means you're inviting them to check in now and then. You'll feel better, and so will they. You might even learn something—and they might, too. How cool is that?

## Connecting with Your Dead

Despite what many mediums claim, the dead aren't always with us. They are resting up, exploring what their souls have been up to and might want to do next, and having new experiences, including traveling the world and other planets. In short, they're busy. So are you. We all move on. We have to.

You can still schedule time for a visit. Work with a professional medium or follow these steps to create a ritual to connect on your own:

- Learn how your intuition works, or risk missing them entirely. That is, if you're expecting to see your dead and your intuition doesn't run toward seeing, game over. If it does, ask to see them. Strong on hearing? Ask them to talk. You feel things? Ask them to share their emotions. If you just know, you'll probably feel silly, so trust that you'll get something unexpected, because you will—eventually.

- Get organized. Prepare a brief, specific list of thoughts and questions beforehand.

- Set a time to connect: for example, ten minutes on a Saturday afternoon.

- At the appointed time, start with a prayer, mantra, something that creates sacred space around you.
- Spend a few minutes quietly relaxing your mind.
- Get yourself grounded and balanced: I use crystals (and common sense), but whatever you do, make sure you are calm, collected, and relaxed.
- Get spiritual protection and support: call a spirit guide to filter out unpleasantries like the random dead. Call in the teams of your beloveds, too.
- Ask your questions. Wait for an answer that hits intuitively. Maybe you'll get one, maybe you won't, at least at first. Or you might get one of those odd duck mysterious "signs" that just clicks. For example, your beloved might have been fond of hummingbirds, and during your ritual, one suddenly buzzes your window. Coincidence, or your beloved teasing you? You decide.
- Be respectful. Remember your dead are off on a new life, even if they haven't reincarnated. Sure, they sometimes check in with you, but you are living your life, and they're living their afterlives. So get to it. Don't expect them to read your mind: that's rude. If you're lucky, they might be patient. Or they might decide you still don't get whatever you didn't get whenever it was and that they now have better things to do—and they'll go do them. Consider yourself warned.
- Sit for whatever time you allotted (or walk in a quiet place, if moving helps you quiet your mind better). When the time is up, thank yourself, all the spiritual teams, and your beloveds for whatever you got, even if you didn't notice anything. If you repeat this exercise often enough, you just might. Okay, I'm pretty sure you will. Somehow.

- End with a mantra or prayer that closes the sacred space you've opened for your ritual and makes you feel that it is complete. Because it is.

- Afterward, decompress with a salt bath or dry salt bathing (running your hands down your body and "shaking" them off over a bowl of sea salt). Salt is an ancient cleansing tool that helps us clear out stuck energy and keep healthy energy flowing. Also, drink lots of water and spend some time relaxing, processing, and being awed by your achievement. Because you really truly actually did it: you connected with your beloveds.

You can do this ritual anywhere, but consider spending time in a dedicated space with an altar that holds mementos, crystals, flowers, photos, fishing lures, baseballs, whatever feels good to you—and you think your beloveds would appreciate. Or get a kick out of. Or both.

### Clear Your Space

Whether you want to honor the dead, your ancestry, or the world for making a place for you in it, plan to keep your home space energetically clear. While space clearing is an involved subject, know that it is especially important in helping to create a nurturing space to help you connect with your dead. Over time you will notice that ritual spaces feel sacred (like ancient churches, holy sites, and my favorites: old-growth forests, ocean beaches, and Yellowstone National Park).

Here are the basics for clearing your space:

- Thank your space daily for providing comfort and security.
- Give your space a present: buy or make something that honors it (like a colorful ribbon).
- Start your ritual: dress up, play music, light candles, call in your spiritual team, say a prayer or mantra.

- Make good use of clearing tools, including incense, herbs, essential oils, sea salt, Himalayan salt lamps, flowers, lavender, crystals, and whatever else feels good. They keep the space clear and remind you that you are choosing to include more mystical or spiritual things in your space because the universe is bigger, and more awesome, than you know—and your dead just might be watching.
- Thank yourself and your spiritual team for joining you.
- End the ritual with a bell, mantra, prayer—again, whatever feels good.

## Grieving as Life Moves On

Mix and match the tips I've offered as you see fit, because the plain, simple truth is that death is the ultimate test of love, no matter which side of it we're on, and we each work through it in our own unique way.

We struggle to say goodbye even when we have the time, but it's especially difficult if the approaching death is sudden or you're rattled by an emergency. Whatever choice you make—if you're lucky enough to make one, instead of having death suddenly drop on your doorstep—do everything possible to logically, rationally, emotionally, physically, and spiritually be at peace with it. Regrets are unnecessary—they can also kill you. If your beloved dies suddenly, know that terrible things happen, make peace with it, and go on. If you did the best you could with whatever you had, it's enough. If you didn't, you'll know better next time. That's what life is—next times.

Grief—well, you know grief never ends. Grief hurts—it's gut-wrenching, soul-testing pain. When grief is overwhelming, it seems impossible and even naïve to think that it could be good, but it is. Grief reminds us that we loved and were loved. Grief reminds us that we care, that we don't live in isolation, that community is everywhere. Grief reminds us that if we didn't grieve, we would never have lived the wonderful life we did with our beloveds, even in the hard times. Grief reminds us that love matters, always and forever.

I believe that if I can do something, anyone can. That's why I know that you can heal grief and live on, even if sometimes, when the pain is devastating, you don't really want to. It will never stop hurting, but it will get better. Someday you'll be able to breathe again, to laugh and enjoy life again. It might even start at your beloved's funeral!

I have suffered devastating losses, and as much as I want my beloveds back, I know that won't happen, not in the bodies I loved so much. So I live the best life I can, full of optimism, peace, humor, and passion. You can, too. Believe it. One day you'll wake up and realize that you did exactly that. I promise you, you will.

Keep remembering that. It helps.

# Parting Words

We're always hearing about love. We think we get it, but we're so caught up in our busy lives that we rarely stop to consider what love really is or how we can embrace it to be our best selves. Besides, deep down we often doubt we're worthy. We carry those feelings into death, where we discover we're still human, still insecure, still wondering if we're good enough—if we're brave enough to wonder at all. We just don't easily embrace our humanity, in all its quirks and foibles, in all its magnificent possibilities.

It's puzzling, really, because we demonstrate love daily, in all the little ways that make a life, from a simple smile for a tired stranger to enjoying a sunset. We're patient with imperfection—unless it's our own. We can always find one more reason to not love ourselves.

Self-love is the key to life—and death. Embracing the no-nonsense, all-important job of loving ourselves, before and after death, is the most important thing we can learn from the experiences of the dead. Choosing love as our guiding principle helps us claim fearless, joyful, confident lives and wise deaths that keep our souls moving forward in their eternal adventures.

Death is a doorway to another experience, one that is enriched by living our lives full-out, mistakes front and center. What will you do with this knowledge? How will you create the passionate life that is your road map to the "after" party my dad raves about? How will you help loved ones claim their own empowered lives and deaths? Easy: one step at a time, starting with loving yourself first.

I believe we must set aside our current religious and cultural constructs and embrace how the world really works: as an equal partnership with all life, which removes the blocks of inferiority, superiority, and control that plague us. However, mindset changes take time, and many people throughout history have done quite well within these constructs, including my own family. Choose what works for you, which always means whatever puts self-love front and center.

Death is a mystery. I doubt we'll know everything about it even after we've safely moved on. Not to worry, though. We don't know everything about life, either.

Losing a beloved is heart-rending. The loss, the grief, the doubts, the worry can derail us. Sometimes we need not just closure, but relief from the devastation. We need to know about the dead. I hope I've helped you understand what happens when we die, so you're prepared for your own death and comforted about a beloved's.

Please say your farewells before you or someone you love dies. If you can't, say goodbye as soon as you learn they've died. While you don't need a medium to connect, consider consulting one if it feels useful, good, and right to get help, reassure yourself that your beloveds are okay, find out what they're up to, resolve whatever concerns you have, relieve your grief and theirs, and get closure.

Conversations with the dead can be glorious, reminding us why love is so important, and inspiring us to keep moving forward. They can also be tough when both sides need to say things they couldn't or didn't say before, because that *is* how we keep moving forward.

Whatever your situation, say what you need to say to put an

end to grief and speculation, including confusion, anger, and hurt, so you can move on. Maybe they'll hear you and whatever you've said will help them advance, if they're ready for that. Remember, here and in the afterlife, souls keep growing. Your job is to first take care of your own.

Try saying something like this, however the combination works for you: Hello. I'm sorry you're dead. I miss you. I don't miss you. I have some real issues with you. Please explain yourself. You were a complete jerk when you were alive and you *still* are; I'm so done with that, goodbye. You were wonderful, I really do miss you. I love you. I have closure now. Goodbye.

A loving farewell helps you and your beloveds. So does releasing guilt, hurt, and anger by giving the dead their crap back to deal with in their afterlife. Sometimes that's how both sides learn and grow. Honesty helps you own your power, allowing true healing to occur.

In all your conversations with your dead, be kind to them and to yourself even as you settle the tough stuff. Be honest. Be respectful. Be you. State the facts and leave it there, because you're not in the same realm anymore: you're alive and they're not, and no matter what, both sides move on in different ways. If they've had any growth from their life review—and most of the dead I talk with have—they already know their mistakes and just want to let you know that, or even apologize, like my dad did when he first showed up so many years ago.

Sometimes, no matter how hard you try, you can't connect with your dead, either with a medium or on your own. We don't always know why. It can mean the dead have issues they're dealing with and they can't talk, they're busy, they're stuck and can't move on, they don't understand the message, or they have chosen not to connect. My dad's ability to connect the living and the dead is rare for way station managers, so maybe other managers you might meet don't know how to facilitate this (although my dad and I are busy training them, so there you go). If you try connecting and nothing happens, keep trying until it does or you decide you're fine without it.

Now, one more thing. People say that the dead are always with you, but do you really want that? Do they?

Besides, it's not true. The dead are not always with you—and they shouldn't be. They are, after all, dead. If you hold on to them too hard, they won't move on to their next opportunity as easily, or they'll be reluctant to talk with you. Remember, their new reality is far different from the life they shared with you. They're off reviewing their lives with their spirit guides, working hard to grow their souls, exploring reality outside of their bodies, playing in different dimensions, goofing off, having adventures, and moving on to other work, maybe even other bodies. Let them do that. Let them move on. You move on. It's life. Really, it's life.

You'll be okay, and so will they. Love makes all things possible, including saying goodbye to someone you can't imagine living without, but have to.

For now.

Yes, for now, because truth is, most of us have been around before and are probably coming around again, if not here on this planet, then somewhere. If you don't choose a physical body, human or not, you have a whole lot of choices by remaining in spirit. Whatever your next choice, you may not remember the specifics of your previous lives, or your times between lives, at least not without some kind of past life regression. But there is one true thing we all know: we remember enough, because we keep choosing love, or at least trying to. In the end, that *is* enough.

You matter.

The dead matter.

Love matters.

Peace.

# Acknowledgments

The world is a better place because we help each other. I am eternally grateful (and I do mean eternally) to the people in my life who encouraged me and helped me be my best, from my medical team throughout the years to family, friends, readers, clients, and social media connections. You all inspire and delight me: never forget how much you matter.

Thanks to my deceased dad, Ray, who asked me to work with him as a medium to help the living and the dead connect, and all those billions of stuck dead move on to the afterlife.

Thanks to the dead who continue to share their stories.

Thanks to my clients, who trust in my unique intuitive and healing skills and methodology. My particular thanks to those who generously agreed to share their sessions in the healing stories. I am honored by their trust, which is humbling, and by their desire to help others by sharing their stories. This … this is why love rules.

My thanks to Christopher Buck and Liane Buck who are OMTimes Media. They generously welcomed me into the fold and shared their wisdom and friendship: my life is better because they are in it. Thanks to Betsy Bergstrom, who first introduced me to the connection between the five elements and the stages of dying. Thanks to Grandma Jody, grandma to all my animals, an outstanding intuitive and medium, and a valued partner in my work. Thanks to Ann Reid, friend and writer. Thanks to all those who've supported my writing, from editorial to marketing to reviews.

Thanks to my amazing production team, friends and brilliant creatives: Robert Lanphear of Lanphear Design; Mary Van de Ven, photographer; and Laurel Robinson, copyeditor.

Thanks to my beloved animal family members, who were coming back to me long before I knew it. To those who are gone and always missed: Maggie, Murphy, Alki, Tweety, and Grace the Cat. To their adorable and rascally new incarnations: Oliver the Cavalier King Charles spaniel and Kerys the Russian Blue cat. Because love is enough.

Life is a tough and hilarious ride: we thrive with good humor, compassion, honest talk, and love in all its messy glory.

# About the Author

Robyn M Fritz MA MBA CHt is an intuitive and spiritual consultant and certified past life regression specialist with a worldwide practice based in Seattle, Washington. She offers intuitive insight and healing services for clients worldwide, including mediumship, personal and business intuition, animal communication, space clearing, past life and between life regression, soul progression clearing, spiritual awakening, and crystal energy healing.

While all her work is a visionary balance of the practical and mystical, her mediumship practice is unique: it's a partnership with her deceased dad, Ray, which was not only his idea, but he insisted on it (parents are like that, even dead ones). Together they help the living and the dead have honest-to-goodness real conversations that resolve grief and get closure while also helping the stuck dead move to the afterlife.

An award-winning writer, magazine columnist, and international radio host, Robyn teaches an inclusive mindset that helps humans thrive as equals with all life while working to become their best selves. She teaches people to embrace their innate intuitive and healing skills while emphasizing self-love, because there's never too much of that in the world. Well aware that there are more things going on in the world than we know, she is all too familiar with most of them. That's why she swears by good humor, compassion, and curiosity, which will help us help the world save itself.

Robyn laughs, loves, and lives near salty Puget Sound with her reincarnated animal family: Oliver Alki, a Cavalier King Charles spaniel, and Kerys, a Russian Blue cat. Find her at robynfritz.com.

www.ingramcontent.com/pod-product-compliance
Lightning Source LLC
Chambersburg PA
CBHW030528010526
44110CB00048B/784